1 MONTH OF
FREE
READING

at

www.ForgottenBooks.com

By purchasing this book you are eligible for one month membership to ForgottenBooks.com, giving you unlimited access to our entire collection of over 1,000,000 titles via our web site and mobile apps.

To claim your free month visit:

www.forgottenbooks.com/free178895

ISBN 978-0-483-22319-6
PIBN 10178895

A DIAGNOSIS

AND OTHER POEMS

BY

WILLIAM PEGRAM

BOSTON

SHERMAN, FRENCH & COMPANY

1916

To those who, in an age conspicuous for its materialism, are, by the more practical-minded, referred to as the " Dreamers "— those Idealists who have succeeded in freeing their minds from the conventional shackles of thought and who, unhampered by the dead hand of tradition and the benumbing touch of superstition and conventional dogmatism, find their real joy and inspiration, and refresh and strengthen their souls, in the contemplation of life's immeasurable possibilities, firm in the conviction that any seeming fault lies not in the plan but rather in ourselves and in our inability to rightly sense the purpose — this little volume is dedicated.

CONTENTS

LIMITATIONS

How mighty, yet how weak, the spoken word!
Strange paradox, so oft in nature found,
This mighty weakness — this weak strength —
    conferred
By Mother Nature upon vocal sound!

At times like lightning flash, in words of fire
The living thoughts conveyed by human speech
Uplift or sink, discourage or inspire,
And round the earth reverberating reach;
Firing, perchance, in some responsive heart,
Stirring a cord in some receptive brain
That loses self and strives to do its part
To see, advance, to conquer and attain!

And yet how weak are words e'en to convey
Primal emotions which our senses thrill!
How much remains which we would fain portray,
Deep sunk in silence, unexpressed and still!
Can we describe the fragrance of the rose,
The after-glory of the western sky,
The beauty that the opening buds disclose,
The inspiration of true harmony?
The cooling draught to one on desert sands,
The faint, caressing, touch of infant hands —
Can words convey the strange, ecstatic bliss
Distilled and held within the lover's kiss?
Each moment of our lives our senses bring
Across the void, and in the brain implant,

Some wireless message caught upon the wing —
The sense-response to outward stimulant.
Each breath we draw but leaves its own impress
Upon the mind, as 'pon the living soul,
Inspiring joy, indifference, distress —
But e'er, in one or other, taking toll!
How many such sensations ne'er arise
Above the surface of our consciousness!
How few that do can we at all devise
To clothe in words, their likeness to impress!
Sensations, these, above the power of speech;
Beyond the spoken, or the written, word;
Which only our self-consciousness can reach —
Self-sensed, indeed, but ne'er by others heard!
How much we feel that we can never fill
Into the mould of words — try as we will!
How many the sensations that abound
Beyond the reach of pen or vocal sound!
And these, our senses, but an octave space
In Nature's keyboard, can no other be
Than five brief chords wherewith, indeed, to trace
The height and depth of Nature's harmony!
With five weak keys might we as well essay
The tones of some grand symphony portray,
As run the gamut of all Nature's scale
With our five senses, limited and frail!
What heights of tone above — what depths
    below —
The furthest point to which our reach may go!
What range of sight our vision fails to tell!

What worlds, indeed, of touch and taste and
    smell!
Who knows but that the flowers, as they grow,
Sing songs of joy — glad hymns of praise re-
    hearse,
Or that, from seeming silence, may not flow
The rhythmic music of the universe?
What depths of feeling and what heights of
    thought
Lie yet in store — far on upon the way!
With what potential powers, indeed, are fraught
The limitations of our present day!
Silence and darkness are the veils that she —
Our Mother Nature — draws about us still!
This much we hear — so far alone we see —
Until our destiny we here fulfill!
Naught but a fragment of the mighty whole
That evolution must at last unroll!
No more than this, but, even so, how great
An inspiration to aspiring soul!

THIS world of men into three camps is split;
The Thoughtless, Skeptic and Idealist.
But of the three, the first should be the last,
For though in number greater far than both
The others, still his kind is such
That he must follow and can never lead.
His is the sort that troubles not to think;
For thinking troubles, and all things that do,
Must, by the constitution of his brain,
Be pushed aside, cast out, or clean forgot.
His is the mind that centres on this life;
He cannot raise his eyes from off the ground;
The service of the senses is his aim,
His one ambition and complete desire.
Life is a balance sheet — profit and loss —
Where all the values are material;
Where: "What the cost?" or "What I thereby
        gain?"
Is all the thought the subject seems to claim.
He dwells not in the future, nor the past;
The thought of neither, contemplation stirs;
The one seems dead and gone and long forgot;
Impious, the other, e'en to think upon.
Believes, if so indeed it may be called,
That which, before him, all his forbears did;
The false and true are both to him alike,
So that they but be sanctified by Time.
Tradition is the god he truly serves,
The god that rules him in the realm of Thought.

[4]

No folly that Tradition passes on,
But claims the homage of his willing knee;
No truth, however pure, or plain, or clear —
However balanced with the soul's desires —
But is fit subject for his mirth and scorn
Without Tradition's stamp and guaranty.
Thus doth the dead hand reach from out the grave
And lay its chilling fingers on the brain
Of him who worships at Tradition's shrine.

Far less in number is the Skeptic's camp,
For to belong to it, he needs must think;
And thinking upon things abstract and vague
Is food too shadowy for the concrete mind,
Depending on a coarser fare to suit
The coarser implement by which it lives
On this, the plane of the Material.
The Skeptic's thought above the earth is raised;
'Tis tied not to the past, nor dreads the future;
Indeed, some shred of reverence were good
To keep his mind from being self-absorbed
And doubting all that is in heaven or earth,
Save but himself — of whom he has no doubts.
His self-esteem is wonderful to see;
" All things to me are known! " he seems to say;
" What is. What is not. And what cannot be! "
And thus, dogmatic'ly, pursues his way.
With scissors and with puny measuring-rod
He clips and measures all that doth exist
In heaven or earth, in sea, or land, or sky,
To fit the cramped conception of his brain,

Saying: "Thus is! Nor else can any be!"
He thinks; indeed, pregnant his mind with
    thought,
But his ideals are strangled at their birth
By the entangling cord of egotism,
And lifeless come the children of his brain
Because they lack the spirit and the soul
Which give the life unto the thing itself.
But still he thinks, and therefore doth he live,
Howe'er devoid of living progeny.
Could he but grasp that little, vital truth —
The truth that all he knows is still not all —
How it would help to vitalize his thought
And stir to life the product of his brain!

The third and last, and yet, indeed, the first —
He, the Idealist! The Dreamer! He
In number is in sad minority;
In volume small, but great in quality!
Each man of them a leader is, in fact;
Thoughtful, reliant, self-controlled and brave;
And needs he must be, for the arms of both
The others are against him turned.
He tempts them not to battle, but he'd die
Before relinquishing his privilege
To see Life truly through his eye of faith —
Faith in his ideals, in himself, in all,
As but faint indications of a truth
Towards which all tending is, in time, revealed.
He traces in his mind the upward path
Leading from faint amœba up to man —

A weary journey by our puny gauge,
But by Eternity a trifling span
That is and is not as we think thereon,
So brief the time of its duration.
And, thinking on't, he needs, in fact, believe
That Man as now conceived is not the goal —
The final goal, at least, that is to say —
Towards which all life has tended up till now.
And if, indeed, his mind be logical,
And Reason by Emotion not controlled,
He must perceive that Nature makes no jumps,
But patiently pursues her endless way
A'down the vista of eternal time.
As through the æons man has been built up
In body, mind and soul to what he is,
As the stalactite, hanging in its cave,
Took countless ages to produce itself,
So must the growth continue, slow but sure,
Throughout the reaches of all future time.
The Thoughtless says he is by this deprived
Of a reward his forbears promised him.
To him, the state of Death would seem a purge
Whereby he is discharged of earthly sin
And all his nature thereby perfected.
If such indeed were so, I wonder who
Would, after change, himself but recognize!
But Nature does not move by leaps and bounds,
Nor jump from finite to the Infinite —
From earthly weakness to eternal strength.
"Death is a sleep and an awakening!"
And when we wake, no better and no worse

Than when, indeed, we laid us down to sleep,
With all our imperfections on our souls,
The journey stretches far before us still.
As all things change, indeed, but Change itself —
As naught persists but Mutability —
Why should the scheme be different then than
    now?
Are not the laws of Nature there, as here?
If not, you say, then wherefore say you so?
Why predicate such inconsistency —
Unless, indeed, like some of earth's puffed-up,
You act as Infinite's interpreter?
But to the Thoughtless and the Skeptic too,
The senses seem the final ultimates;
To see, to hear, to taste, to feel, to smell,
The court of last resort — the bench supreme.
To them, what cannot by these measurements
Be gauged, explained, allotted to its sphere,
Cannot exist — as judged by their decree.
But to the Dreamer, all the senses are
But as five puny octaves on the board
That stretches both ways to infinitude.
For in the plan of Nature's harmony
The key-board stretches out continuously ·
From infinite great to still more infinite small;
From worlds compared with which our little globe
Is but a trifling asteroid in space,
To molecule, electron and to atom,
Each one a solar system in itself.
What happens 'neath, or 'bove, the little span
To which his senses furnish him the key,

[8]

How can man say: " This can," or " Cannot
    be "?
Thus to their limit his five senses come;
Beyond the which he is, perforce, estopped
If he would prove what out beyond them lies.
But here the Dreamer, with a finer sense —
That of Perception, true, intuitive —
With vision clear and mind unprejudiced,
Unhampered by opinion preconceived,
With all his spiritual faculties awake,
Reaches beyond the boundary recognized.
He knows that, for this earth and all thereon,
The five material senses are complete;
But also knows, if one would rise from there,
And measure elements as light as air,
He must these higher senses recognize
And then develop to his utmost power.
In doing that he but develops that
Within himself which is himself indeed;
Far more himself than his material form,
A thing unstable and ephemeral,
Which comes and goes within a summer's day.
And while he thus within himself lays up
A treasure greater far than lands or gold,
Who knows but that, perchance, he may alight
Upon a little grain of shining Truth,
As yet unfound by other searchers here,
Which, when more clearly seen by other eyes,
Will add a lustre to their daily lives
Which formerly naught else within them brought?
Thus, with his feet upon the earth, his eyes

Are ever turned unto the cloudless skies,
For there his vision ever beckons on
Towards states of thought and feeling to be won.

A DIAGNOSIS

The ills that soul is heir to.

SHOULD some wise moral doctor but appear —
Some great physician of the human mind,
Diagnostician of the inner man —
What symptoms here within us would he find
Most rampant and productive of that strife
Which saps the very marrow of our life? —
A strife, compared with which the body ills
That flesh is heir to, do but sink and wane
To something insignificant and small —
A passing phase of this the thing called Pain!
For ailments of the body ne'er impress
A lasting stigma on the living soul,
Nor cause that suffering and dire distress
Which, from the heart, demand such heavy toll!

Perchance he'd find Subjection in a few —
That strange paralysis of will and mind
Which e'er must act as it is told to do,
And thus its will to other will but bind! —
An abject state of utter slavery
Which lacks the strength the other to refute,
Controlled by naught but thieving knavery
Which other self, to self, would prostitute!
How sad a state of mind and thought and soul
Thus to renounce its own, its proper, goal,
And thus to place all that which is divine
Beyond the limits of its own control!

But while our learned doctor in his quest
May find some such, he'll find at hand and near
Unnumbered thousands who are all oppressed
By some phase of a strange, malignant Fear.
For many phases has this malady,
To ever teeming offspring it gives birth,
Which find their lodgment in the soul of Man —
These parasites that populate the earth!
For from Despair and Dread, Horror, Dismay —
These lusty children of the parent Fear —
To mere Suspicion and weak Bashfulness,
Or shy Alarm, some of them ever leer
Upon us with their dull, evasive eyes,
Causing an instant chilling of the heart,
And prompting doubt, distrust, or wild surmise,—
A checkened breath, involuntary start!
How many people recognize them all
As products of the one and self-same womb,
Or realize, when subject to their call,
How much their presence robs, of life, the bloom?
For as the budding flower of early May
Is turned by frost to something dull and grey,
So life itself becomes but sad and drear
When haunted by the progeny of Fear!
And though the one be wild, the other tame,
And different means to common end employ,
The net result in all is quite the same
And life is robbed of all its hope and joy,
For all but freeze and paralyze the soul —
Some fast, some slow, but, slowly, just as sure —

And all but lead unto the self-same goal
And render life a thing but to endure!
How many who are otherwise exempt,
To foolish superstition pay a toll!
And though their reason treat it with contempt,
Must thus to some vague Fear make this their
    dole!
Some foolish trick, far back in childhood taught
By Ignorance to Weakness, is their ban!
With such results such things as these are
    fraught!
Such little things as these unman a man!
For superstition can but ever grow
With that 'pon which it feeds, and thus and so,
From small beginnings doth it now and here
Lay the foundations of a greater Fear!
How oft is trusting childhood blindly led —
Sometimes by age, with white and hoary head —
To scan the new moon clearly while he may,
Or suffer from some dim and nameless dread?
'Tis bad enough, and sad enough, forsooth,
To see such lack of reason in old age,
But criminal thus to instil in youth
And leave a blot upon its spotless page!
Refrigeration this! No more, no less!
Psychic refrigeration that doth hold
The life in pawn, and freezingly would dress
All life in its stark, adamantine cold!
Perhaps, of all the many ills of Man,
No other so upsets his every plan,

[13]

Or holds above him such relentless hand
With which to curb, subdue, constrain, command!

This being so, were't not, indeed, but wise
That to this pregnant fact he ope his eyes,
And strive by self-analysis to find
To what extent it dominates his mind?
For if to forewarn is but to forearm,
The knowledge should but strengthen, not alarm,
And thus realization serve to be
The power that puts him 'yond the reach of harm!
But many fail to see to what extent
They are by Fear but twisted, warped and bent;
How large a part it plays within their life;
How, in some phase, it is forever rife!
Forgetting self, it oft becomes alarm
That loved ones may be subject to some harm;
And e'en solicitude becomes a bane,
Bringing mistrust, anxiety and pain.
Thus Apprehension and Anxiety,
Despondency, Timidity and Dread
Are but the offspring of the parent Fear —
Those evil forces which of Fear are bred!
It matters not if for another's sake
We give them lodgment, or permit that they
Control our lives, for, in the final stake,
'Tis our's the loss — as our's the debt to pay!
For they can never but disorganize,
Attack, reduce, destroy, but ne'er defend
That which, within, we should most greatly prize,
And cause disintegration in the end!

Offsetting this, another influence doth
Most frequently within our lives appear —
One that, indeed, is quite the opposite
And the direct antithesis of Fear.
But in some of its many varied shades,
Within us all it plays no minor part,
And oft usurps the centre of the stage,
Affecting mind and soul, as well as heart.
For — unlike Fear that slowly doth congeal,
Doth freeze and paralyze will and desire —
Anger would quite another form reveal
And shows itself as a consuming fire!
Psychic Combustion 'tis! — a withering flame
That sears and scorches both the heart and soul
Of him who bends to its malignant sway
Through weakness or a lack of self-control!
And, even as Fear, it has its many shades
That range from Fury, Desperation, Hate —
From Wrath, Revenge — those violent passions
      which
Their appetites 'pon others crave to sate —
To simple Irritation, Bitterness,
Small Pettishness, Annoyance and weak Pique,
Which claim no bloody victim, but which still
Some small revenge would 'pon another wreak.
All are but scions of the self-same house! —
All Anger's offspring, children of the flame
That burns and withers, and — if slow or fast —
Destruction wrought by each must be the same!
For as in pride the Ancients used to boast
That every road but led at last to Rome,

So here the course, if crooked or if straight,
If but pursued, to the same end must come;
And be the finish far or be it near,
Persistence leads at last unto that goal
That's reached by other ways, indeed, by
    Fear —
Final Annihilation of the Soul!

And from these two there is another ill
Combined, which takes from both of them a part —
That virus which we know as Jealousy,
That deadly poison of the human heart.
For does it not but demonstrate a fear
At losing that which it would call its own,
And anger at th' attempt which prompts re-
    venge
To make another suffer and atone?
This trait'rous thing — this green-eyed Jeal-
    ousy —
Stalks as a spectral shape through many a life,
Curdling the milk of all true charity
And sowing discord, bitterness and strife!

And many suffer from cruel Envy's fangs —
That blighting scourge that cannot contemplate
Another's fortune, but must feel the pangs
Of sorrow, disappointment, and of hate!
That thing which blinds to what we have and
    begs
For what we have not; which must ever dwell

Upon those others — turning but to dregs
The cup of life, and earth into a hell!

And would not this our doctor also find
That Self-Indulgence played a mighty part
In the corruption of the human mind,
The undermining of the human heart?
For Self-Indulgence, of the many things
That sap the soul, the ammunition brings
And lays the plans for the unending strife
Against the very citadel of Life! —
Indulgence of our anger and our fear,
Indulgence of our passions physical,
Indulgence of our mental weaknesses,
Indulgences of states emotional.
For even this, the latter — even that
Emotion which, religious, we profess —
Can by Indulgence be but carried far,
Far down the pathway of destructiveness.
Thus Temperance must be the word that we
Inscribe upon the banner of our soul,
And temperate in all things we must be
In this our progress towards the final goal!
For there's no passion, appetite, desire,
Emotion, impulse, or ambition which
Itself is right, but still that may not be
By Self-Indulgence carried to excess!
And he must be, indeed, both strong and wise —
Must know himself and study well the signs,
Appraise conditions and himself apprize

When they have crossed the true constructive
    lines!
Thus must he ever be upon his guard
Gainst self-indulgence of the many things
That growth of mind and spirit would retard
And which this modern life so often brings.
Mere creature comfort, animal desire,
The thirst for power and might, the greed for
    gold
And for material things, if he aspire
To greater heights, he must indeed withhold;
For he must first be master of himself,
And till he be, he holds no honored place!
And though his coffers be o'ercrammed with pelf,
He has but started in the mighty race!
For he alone is masterful who can
Give latitude, within constructive lines,
To these his impulses, nor mar the plan
By Nature drawn, nor thwart her just designs!

But, in his diagnosis, would not this
Our great physician quickly come to see
How many suffer from another ill —
That all-besetting one called Vanity?
For Vanity, of body or ·of mind,
Is seldom very difficult to find!
And from some phase of it so few are free
'Twould seem almost universality.
Conceit of person, or conceit of mind,
The one, the other, or of both combined —
Whate'er our nation or our parentage —

Would seem to all a common heritage!
The first, of women the besetting sin;
The latter, most monopolized by men;
But both, in both, or in the other, found;
And most luxuriant where least the ground!
It hath, like other ills, full many ways
Of action, and demands that others see,
And in return grant a due meed of praise
That we are e'en as we would seem to be.
Pride of Intelligence and Pride of Thought
With suicidal tendencies are fraught,
Become o'erbearing and give birth to all
That Self-Esteem that topples to a fall!
How very rarely 'tis, indeed, we find
The man prepared to listen, not to preach!
How joyously we welcome such a mind —
The mind that is content to learn — not teach!
For in our self-conceited arrogance,
How many hold to that they really know,
And would not 'pon some other mind impress
That which they merely think is such and so?
How rampant in religion is this fault!
How many creeds are under this, its sway!
How common, Common Truth thus to default
By claiming this, our own, the only way!
If we should Arrogance and Self-Esteem
Denounce as vile, should we expect to search
Here for that simple Charity we deem
The one true offspring of a " Holy Church "?
For, blinded by their self-esteem, can they
Ever true leaders of the blinded be?

While deaf to all but that which they would say —
Steeped in such self-assuring Vanity!
For who, forsooth, can lead that will not learn
And who knows Truth, that Truth, indeed, would
    spurn?
And who of Light can other minds apprize,
Who shuts his own and strives to shut their eyes?
Not all, indeed, do thus so grossly sin,
But many do! And they should bear their part
Of just rebuke, and should, indeed, begin
To search for Truth within the mind and heart.
If they'd assume all Truth is not yet found
And in some ancient treatise firmly bound,
And search for it within the living soul,
They might, indeed, come nearer to the goal!
Perchance if charity of thought they'd sow,
Such planting might to fuller harvest grow,
And teeming granaries replace those, now,
Which ever-dwindling store indeed but show!
If from Tradition's drying carcass they
Would strive to loose, as now they strive to bind,
Can any doubt that the result would pay
In strengthened heart and spirit, soul and mind?
For how can living prosper with the dead,
Or Thought advance when by Tradition led?
And how can thirsty mind succeed to drink,
When Truth is shunned and brain denied to
    think?
God gave us brains to think and minds to use,
And if we fail to, we His gifts abuse,
For Self-Deceit is nothing but deceit,

Nor any less if fathered by Conceit!
Therefore is Vanity indeed a curse
In many ways 'twere needless to rehearse;
And if we be but honest, we must see
That from some form at least we're seldom free!
Thus is it ever best to fully ope'
Our eyes to Truth — distasteful though it be —
For herein lies salvation and true hope —
Salvation from a dense obscurity!
Pride — proper pride — in what we are and do,
True self-respect — not self-complacency —
If rightly earned, is nothing but our due
And will not flower in self-sufficiency!
For is the soul not able to decide
When it is right?   And is not worthy pride
And self-respect and proper self-regard
But Nature's due and merited reward?
But we must e'er be honest with ourselves,
And study self as if a thing apart,
Nor let blind, selfish sophistry create
Fictitious reasons for the mind and heart!

And yet one other ill, at least, would not
Our great physician find? — A slow disease
That eats the very vitals of the heart
And mind and soul of him whom it doth seize?
As Anger is combustion, and as Fear
In slow refrigeration takes its toll,
Self-Pity, so pathetic, weak and drear,
Is but consumption of the living soul!
A psychic phthisis, dull and desolate,

That slow but surely ever eats its way
Into the soul of him who harbors it
And turns all life into a dismal grey!
'Tis largely based upon assumption that
His, of all others, are the greatest hurts —
That God, or Nature, or Intelligence,
Withholds from him alone his just deserts!
With Envy, shares conviction of the fact
That others have what to him is denied,
And this but poisons every thought and act
And comes at last to be a cause of pride —
Pride that his own misfortunes are so great,
So greater, far, than any have to bear,
Pride in his misery, his weakened state
Of which he thinks no other is aware!
A thing debasing, sickly, weak and mean;
Containing nothing of virility;
That cannot see, though yet by others seen,
That it leads straight to imbecility!
He sues for pity, understanding, help;
Demands that all should listen to his wail
And sympathize with his misfortune; and
Where'er he goes he leaves his slimy trail —
A trail that, first inspiring but distrust,
At last inspires but nausea and disgust;
A trail whose stenches vitiate the air
And render it impossible to bear!
And ever is his cry for sympathy,
Full understanding of his awful woe,
Ne'er recking that his course but dries the spring
From which true sympathy must ever flow,

But like a pestilential plague he goes,
Spreading contagion of his fancied woes
And thus, self-blinded, e'er pursues his course
And checks the stream of love e'en at its source!
For happiness to these can never be,
Unless unhappiness they ever spread;
And, being bound, they would but bind the free
To this their selfish misery and dread!
'Tis marvelous the stock of misery
That from one such as this can be derived,
And the amount of joy and gaiety
Of which this life by one can be deprived!
Of all the plagues that human life may gall,
This drivelling weakness seems the worst of all!—
This thing devoid of shame, from hope exempt;
Beyond all sympathy; beneath contempt!
If such as these would their possessions gauge
By their deserts, perchance it might assuage
This selfish pity and assist to show
How little owed, compared with what they owe!
Perchance these martyrs constitutional
Would cease their wailing and unending strife,
Becoming debtors restitutional
To these, their suffering fellows and to life.
No doubt possessions balance our deserts,
For what the first but that which Man converts
From out of life, and makes a conscious part
Of this, his mind and brain and soul and heart?
For all men's efforts point to but one end;
To all alike is Happiness the goal

And naught esteemed that does not towards this
    tend —
This the unerring instinct of the soul!
But many but mistake what this will bring,
And all their time and effort blindly fling
Into some cause which, when achieved and past,
They find but dust and ashes at the last!
And thus the man whose object is but gold,
May pile up wealth and riches manifold,
To find that Happiness itself has fled
To him who labors for his daily bread!
For Happiness is not bound up in wealth,
In power, in station, or in body health,
But may be found in one, in all these poor,
Who yet of it doth hold a goodly store.
What is it but contentment of the mind? —
An attitude of soul that still can find —
Without these strange necessities of Man —
A conscious harmony with Nature's plan?
For, to possess at all, we needs must use —
And use aright — else we do but abuse
These same possessions which, indeed, but goad,
With obligation added to the load!
Thus, to receive, we also have to give,
For who that does not, can be said to live?
And this same giving ne'er depletes our store,
But ever brings us riches more and more!
And gifts are gifts, no matter what they be,
If that they be but that which others need —
Not what they crave, but that which one can
    see

Will, if but planted, come to flowering seed.
A little sympathy, a kindly word,
A just appreciation of the worth,—
But little things, indeed, though seldom heard,
And, though so cheap, conspicuous by their
     dearth!
Sometimes, indeed, a little word of cheer,
A hearty grasp of such a friendly hand,
May change a prospect desolate and drear,
And cause a drooping spirit to expand!
How little means a legacy of gold,
Bequeathed by the necessity of death,
If favors such as these we would withhold
Which cost us nothing but a little breath!
A little breath, a little kindly thought,
A little effort, and some self-control —
With what a store of wealth, indeed, are fraught
These, the donations of the living soul!
'Tis this penuriousness that doth offend
In those who in self-pity ever live;
For they'd receive forever without end,
Nor recognize at all the need to give.
And true perception of this fault alone,
Within the soul, but prompts that we atone
Therefor by shutting up or draining dry
The flood of sympathy for which they cry.

Thus have we tried, if faultily, to scan
These the most common sicknesses of Man,
Which would be found in part, if not in whole,
By some diagnostician of the soul.

And few, if any, would be found quite free —
Howe'er they seem, or would appear to be —
Of some such symptom, be it strong or faint,
That would to him portray their true complaint.
But many to such symptoms would be blind;
Would fail to look, or — looking — fail to find;
And thus, self-blinded, gain a fleeting ease,
But leave unchecked a ravaging disease!
Thus do the thoughtless, ignorant and crude,
E'en as the ostrich when by Man pursued,
They hide their eyes and stifle their alarm
And think thereby they have escaped all harm!
But such self-blindness never served its end;
It serves but to disarm, not to forefend.
Realization of a fault must first
Supply material with which to mend.

Then would not this, our doctor, first insist
That this, our case, can offer little hope
Until self-blindness firmly we resist
And grant to self-analysis full scope?
And would not also his prescription be
That thought and mind must function full and
    free —
Unbound, unhampered, by Tradition's hand,
Untrammelled by conventional demand?
And as a tonic would not he decide
That temperance in all must be our guide —
Our watchword and our stay in time of need,
Our gauge to measure thought and speech and
    deed —

And 'neath this even our emotions bring,
Which, left unchecked, would this our reason fling
Out of its course, deprive of all command,
And headlong run, without a guiding hand?
And would not Temperance, if thus pursued —
Thus supplicated, importuned and wooed —
Give birth at last, indeed, to Self-Control —
That prime essential of the growing soul?
For Self-Control, once born, will grow in strength,
In power, in scope, in knowledge, till at length
It quite o'ercomes these ills and sets Man free
To be what Nature meant that he should be!
And thus Subjection, Anger, Envy, Fear,
Self-Pity, Self-Indulgence, Vanity —
Of mind or body — also Jealousy,
Will from his constitution disappear!
Then — and then only — is he truly free!
Then — and then only — can he clearly see!
Then will he but conform to Nature's Plan!
Then — not till then — can he be called a Man!

THE REGENERATION

Of all the ages since the world began —
Cleft, subdivided to that little span
Allotted unto man — would seem to be
The present fraught with possibility!
A generation, this, that stands beyond
All generations that have gone before;
More fraught with change, deep and significant;
More large and pregnant with a coming life;
More full of thought and feeling infinite
Than any other since the birth of Time —
Of Time, that is, applied to things known here;
For who can say that in the lapse of time
Whereof our own is but a moment's breath,
In other worlds, as yet to us unknown,
The very forces that are rampant now
Have not the battle fought, 'gain and again?
Who, pray, are we that we should predicate
That this, our little world, is of them all
The first, the one and only, battle ground
Whereon the forces Good and Evil wage
That fierce and bloody, that unending, fight —
Begun, no doubt, e'en with the birth of Time,
And doubtless to be fought till Time shall end?
But now and here, upon this mundane sphere,
Forces are loose and actively at work
Such as were never known by man before
So far as history guides our reckoning!
Is it, perchance, the harvest we have sown?
The reaping of the crop material?

The true and just fruition of that fruit
Which we have nurtured with material lives?
In thoughtless pride and puny arrogance;
In egotism and in self-conceit;
In thought alone of power, esteem and wealth; —
Have we, perchance, but undermined the health
Of mind, of body and of soul as well,
Until with some the soul has pined and died?
Such are, or such at least would seem to be,
They who stake all upon material force;
Who think the only law The-Will-to-Have,
When backed and strengthened by The-Will-to
    Hold;
Who dream not of the rights of other men —
Their thoughts, their feelings, or their soul's de-
    sire —
But only of themselves, and how, and when
They can but gain that to which they aspire!
The god Material Force they have enshrined,
To whom they humbly bend the knee and pray;
Those that agree with them are friends, opined;
But, execrated, those who block the way!
'Gainst these are now arrayed another class —
Not blameless all, nor yet, indeed, quite free
Of that same scourge, the plague Materialism,
But feeling 'neath their superficial lives
The swelling of that other mighty Force,
The birth-pains of that new Idealism
Which throbs their pulses, quickening in their
    souls
The strong conviction that Man must be free!

Free to pursue his own, his native course,
In thought, in action and in government,
Without coercion and extraneous force,
Towards that goal — his greatest own content!
Life; liberty; pursuit of happiness!
The rights inalienable of each soul!
No more should man possess; and never less
Must be his object and his final goal!
And here and now they wage the bitter fight —
The God Material, the God of Power,
Against that other god — the God of Right!
And as they rage, the heavens darkly lower
And over all the world has spread a gloom
As though presaging now the Day of Doom!
Wars still!   And rumors, still, of other wars!
And nation against nation has arisen!
And people against people! Yea! in lands
As yet not risen in embattlement!
Nor yet are signs and portents far to seek —
The signs of great and deep and broad unrest,
The portent of illimitable surge,
Of flux and change and constant ebb and flow
Throughout the masses of humanity!
And few men know their neighbors, or their
    friends,
For brother against brother is offset;
And no man knows what each day's sun may
    bring,
Nor what tomorrow has in store for him!
What mean these signs, these portents of the
    times,

These frank misgivings and this doubt of self,
Which make us hesitate to say: " I know!"
Knowing how little 'tis, indeed, we know?
What mean, I say, these questions and this doubt,
This sorrow and this suffering o'er the earth,
Unless it be intended but to flout
Our petty self-conceit and mark the birth
Of new conceptions and idealism?
For greater birth-pains here have ne'er been felt;
They must, it seems, some greater birth presage
Than e'er delivered yet this Earth has been!
Some birth portentous, high, serene, alone
Could compensate for these pre-natal pains
Which otherwise would seem to mock and jeer
Our puny efforts and ambitions here!
A silver lining has indeed the Time
Which otherwise seems overwrought and sad,
For in the heart and soul of every man
The little, active leaven is at work,
Making him think what ne'er he thought before;
Withdrawing from himself his constant gaze,
And rivetting the heart and soul of him
Upon conceptions of the Right and Wrong,—
Upon the ideals born within himself,
Which, up till now, indeed, were yet still-born
And had not quickened into active life!
Such is the Time! And such the lesson we
Can master, if we have but eyes to see
And ears to hear and brains, indeed, to think,
While nation wars with nation on the brink
Of what seems now an awful precipice!

And therefore thank I now that Higher Power
That hath permitted me the present hour
In which to draw my little span of breath,
E'en if, by doing so, I must, by death
Upon the battle-field, relinquish it!
For what more fitting end to earthly life
Than render it again in final strife
Against the Power of Wrong, and, in the fight,
Die that I may but help uphold The Right?

LIFE CONTINUOUS

THERE is no death if by that word you mean
The change of " being " into something " been,"
" Is " into " was," and " present " into " past,"
And " passing life " to " life already passed "!
For what, this life, but the initial school —
The kindergarten, so to speak, of Man,
Of conscious Man, who here must learn the rule
Of what he cannot do, and what he can?
For many ages in the nursery
Were passed e'er mind and soul became so strong
That Man was conscious of his consciousness —
Fit to distinguish 'twixt the Right and Wrong!
And so this present life is but the test
Wherein our knowledge and experience
Prompt to such action as to us seems best
Wherewith to gain the proper recompense
For all that we have felt and done while here!
But here the way is somewhat hard to see,
And things appear not as they really be;
Emotion here is checked by Reason there;
And Reason and Emotion must compare
With Conscience as the final arbiter!
Our obligations and our rights we learn,
Both to ourselves and to our fellow man;
The which to give, the which, again, to spurn,
To check our lives by the eternal plan
Which Nature has laid down as her decree!
And with our dispositions manifold —
Our strength, our weakness, our heredity,

The tempt' to lust, to power, the tempt' of gold —
The way is very often hard to see
And we are lost in great perplexity!
Here in the school of life we are to seek
The lessons Life can teach to every one,
Convert to strength that which within is weak,
And learn our utmost e'er the day be done!
And when from out this school we graduate
Unto another, we continue there
The self-same progress and development
On the foundations we but started here!
What else could mean this life's experience,
This progress, this advance of mind and soul,
If it, indeed, were something separate
And not but part of the same mighty whole
That stretches forward to Eternity?
What mocking of our earnest efforts here,
If we were not the due reward to gain
Of these same efforts, or had cause to fear
That all had been but useless waste and pain!
I would not so insult Intelligence —
The Great Intelligence, or e'en that part
Of it which is contained within each soul
And quickens to the beating of each heart.
For 'twould indeed be but a sorry jest
Thus to reach out the cup unto the lips
But to withdraw and dash our hopes when we
Had all but clasped it with our finger tips!

" E'en as ye sow, so, also, shall ye reap!"
Aye! so it is!   And e'en it must be so!

Or else attribute to Intelligence
Motives that are contemptible and low!
And so again I say: There is no death —
No death, at least, such as we oft allow;
But a progressing continuity
That reaches from the present Here and Now,
Unbroken, to the future There and Then!
Again I say: This life is but a part
Of life continuous — that mighty whole
Which, if denied by mind, is not by heart —
And is the aspiration of the soul!

THE GREAT LAW

As everything within this world of ours
And all the kingdoms that it doth include —
If we except, alone, the soul, the mind,
The thought, the " being," the self-conscious-
      ness —
Can, in the final, last analysis,
Unto the simple atom be reduced,
So doth it often seem to me that all
The seeming complex laws that govern us —
Those laws of Nature infinite and great —
Must be resolved at last into but one!
Into one single, great, but simple law,
So great and single that it doth contain
All other laws combined; so simple that
We have o'erlooked it quite, straining our eyes
And meagre brains to find far, far afield
The vital truth that here before us lies.
What law of Nature is it that doth cause
The atom to attract or to repel
Its neighbor atom, deep within the breast
Of cold and flinty rock inanimate?
What law of Nature causes sap to rise
Within the greening branches of the tree,
And makes the opening leaf or flower apprize
Us of a life where life seemed not to be?
What law produces the organic life
Exemplified in animal and man
And from spermatic, microscopic cell
Builds up, upon undeviating plan,

That strange and complicated organism?
What law so works upon all planes of life?
What causes, in the field of Chemistry,
Those same attractions and repulsions which
Give life again to other things that be?
What makes the rain to fall; the wind to blow;
The river ever to the ocean flow;
The stone to drop; the earth, indeed, to turn
Within its orbit round the central sun?
And what, again, that law that doth attract
Body to body; mind to other mind;
And soul, again, unto another soul,
As atom unto atom in the rock?
When long upon the subject the mind thinks
Do not they every one appear to be
Sep'rate, but still united, little links
Within the great chain of Affinity?
By many names this law, indeed, is called,
And many laws, in this one, seem to be.
But what is in the name, whate'er 'tis called,
If we the law itself but plainly see?
'Tis true we see it as " vibration's law,"
Which as a law of science we recognize,
But still, as yet, how dimly do we grasp
All that it means and all that it implies!
For we but set aside a little space
Within the field of Nature for its play,
Saying: " Thus far — no farther — shalt thou
      go!"
As though this law of laws should us obey!
And thus we try to fence and hedge it round;

Refuse to look; or, looking, fail to see
That it doth govern all that doth exist
In heaven or earth, or land, or sky, or sea!
There is a principle in Nature that
Impels each conscious individual
To seek a vibratory correspondence with
Another individual such as he,
But of an opposite polarity.
And through all Nature runs this principle —
Through all the kingdoms up to that of Man,
In which, indeed, it flowers and comes to fruit,
So far as we can know fruition here;
For here attraction is not chemical,
Nor yet alone attraction physical,
But both of these combined and, with them, that
Of mind and soul — attraction spiritual!
Such as it is and great as it may be,
It here can give us but a faint foretaste
Of all that lies in store for us when we
Have graduated to a higher state!
For who can set a limit to the soul
And all the joys that therein dormant lie
When part to part is joined in perfect whole —
A whole complete and pure, serene and high —
A whole comprising perfect unity?
But Time, in its unending course, shall prove
That all things on the earth — in heaven above —
Howe'er unconsciously, obey and move
To this affinity — this Law of Love!

THE OPPORTUNITY TO LEARN

"It is worth noting that the opportunities for which Dr. Abraham Jacobi expressed a sense of obligation on his eighty-sixth birthday, were 'the opportunities to learn.' The young hospital interne doesn't always see it that way."
— *Newspaper clipping.*

A LEARNED doctor once did truly say,
When he had reached unto a ripe old age —
When four score years and six behind him lay
And he reputed as a learned sage —
That of all the earth's opportunities
For which the heart may pine or soul may yearn,
The greatest far, at last, appeared to him
The simple opportunity to learn!

For this he felt an obligation which
Outranked all others that upon him lay,
An obligation unto life, the which
He felt his inability to pay!
If any other word he ne'er had spoke,
And if twice four score were instead his age,
The recognition of this truth alone
Were fit to stamp him as a very sage!
For what, indeed, are opportunities
To wealth, to power, to all for which we burn,
Compared with this — the greatest of them all —
The simple opportunity to learn?
For wealth and power are but a transient phase —
Things that but come and go; a passing breath;
A phantom form, appearing from the haze,

No sooner grasped than lost again by death!
As children, chasing bubbles on the stream,—
Striving to grasp them ere they reach the shore,—
Get for their pains a momentary gleam
And ope' their hands to find they are no more!
But learning is unlike both power and wealth;
Unsought by thieves; untouched by moth or rust;
Free from attack, both open and by stealth;
Unlike our bodies changing back to dust;
For learning is a conscious part of us,
A part of that within which is the whole,
That thing within us which, indeed, is US —
The living, conscious, everlasting soul!

THERE IS NO DEATH!

THERE is no death!
The thing that we call death
Is but a passing cession of the breath!
                    No more!

Afraid to die?
Are you afraid to sleep?
No more therein your consciousness you keep —
                    E'en less!

Afraid to wake?
Are you afraid to ope'
Your eyes to each new day and its new hope?
                    Not so!

Then why fear death?
Its coming rather greet
As portal leading to life more complete
                    Than now!

There is no death!
The thought is but a vain
Phantasmagoria cast upon the brain
                    Of us!

There is no Death!

PAIN

I SOMETIMES think that that which we call " Pain "
Is not a loss, but rather is a gain
If we can find and bring within our reach
The lesson 'tis intended but to teach!
If that our lives conformed to Nature's plan,
And from all evil we should thus abstain,
Would there, indeed, be cause for such a ban,
Or rhyme or reason for the thing called Pain?
Is't not, indeed, the way that Nature hath
Of teaching wisdom to our fleeting day,
Advising when our feet are in the path
And warning when in other ways they stray?
Be it a lack of knowledge, or a fault
Of mind, of reason, or pure physical
Indulgence to some passing, brief desire —
Surrender to a state emotional —
Whate'er the field wherein our fault doth lie,
If contravening one of Nature's laws,
Pain comes to warn us that we must comply
As sure as that effect doth follow cause!
'Tis true that pain from others' faults may come,
And thus bring to our own an added sum,
For we cannot live to ourselves alone,
But must in part for others' faults atone.
Yet in such cases are we always free
Of share in the responsibility —
Our minds so true, our eyes so clear to see
That things are always as they seem to be?
But if with such a fault we have no part —

If it be none of ours, but his in whole —
Does not conviction stir within the heart
And whisper its assurance to the soul?
We suffer, yes! but suffer not as we
Would suffer if the fault within us lay,
For something tells us that of guilt we're free —
Not ours the score to meet, the debt to pay!
Perchance for love we'd gladly share the load
In part or whole, to make another free,
But even then it fails in part to goad,
Being lightened of responsibility.

'Tis this, indeed, that adds the greatest weight
To any load of pain that we may bear,
The which, if conscience doth at all abate,
Is by comparison as light as air!
Is 't not, indeed, a strange provision, this,
Of Nature, which by conscience doth atone
To light a burden that for love we bear —
A burden which, indeed, is not our own?
For though the pain be very great indeed,
And though the journey seem a weary length,
No doubts and fears our footsteps then impede
And we are armed with a new inner strength.
And thus I say that Pain does hold a place
Within the scheme of things, within the plan
Laid out by Nature for the human race,
Developed from the animal to Man!
The brute no conscience has; no right and wrong;
No false and true; no higher loss and gain;
No promptings that above the earth belong,

And without which there can be little pain!
Thus, without Pain, could man indeed be Man?
Is't not, indeed, the hardening alloy
That strengthens character and, in the span
Of this short life, points out the way to joy?
And even here cannot we pain escape —
Much pain, at least — if but in wisdom each
Would so his course of life and action shape
To learn the lesson Nature has to teach?
We cannot, of ourselves, her laws reform
And change what is to what we think should be;
Is't not, then, better freely to conform,
Attempt to look and, looking, strive to see?
'Tis Nature's law and she is ever just;
And recognize it in the end, we must!
Then why not now?   And so convert our pain
From seeming loss to everlasting gain!

CHARITY

What is the meaning of that word which we
So oft and glibly use — that " Charity "?
So much employed, its meaning clear should be,
And one 'pon which all people can agree!
To some it stands for an innocuous state —
A neutral ground, devoid of any hate —
Presided over by the little dove
Of peace — in short, a state of perfect love,
Wherein we're taught to love our enemies,
Respect those who ourselves do but despise,
Return but good for evil done to us,
That thus within us greater good may rise.
Mayhap to these, the few, 'twould bring a boon
In humbleness and self-control that soon
Would blossom forth; but what must we infer
For those, the others — they, the ones that err?
If humbleness and self-control bear fruit
Of passing worth to them that exercise
These virtues, what the crop, forsooth,
Of those who these same virtues but despise?
Will not, indeed, their appetite but grow
With that 'pon which it feeds, and will not so
Their evil instincts more and more control
The ever fainter whisper of the soul?
Is 't by providing drink, indeed, that we
Teach weakness lessons of sobriety?
Or is it, rather, with emphatic " No!
Thus far thou mayest — but no farther — go! "?
Even he — the man we call the Prince of Peace,

Who many the true Son of God profess —
Bowed not before the strength of evil thus,
Or carried Charity to such excess!
Else would the money-changers not have had
Free access to the temple's sacred ground?
And what about the Scribes and Pharisees
'Gainst whom he uttered warnings so profound?
For pride and arrogance and self-conceit
Found ever words appropriate and meet —
Words full of power, reproach and clarity —
But never words of simple charity!
These he kept rather for the poor and weak;
For those who failed, indeed, but still would seek
For something higher than their own desire —
Those who, in short, had souls that could aspire.
'Tis true he taught us not to search the mote
Within our neighbor's eye; but would this seem
Thus truly to imply we should not note
That this, our neighbor's eye, contained the beam?
For thus is good advice oft carried far
Beyond the point that it was meant to go,
Bringing alone confusion to the mind,
And thus converting " Yes " into a " No "!
He who has failed, or sinned, or done aught else
That's possible to man, e'en with intent
To do the same, should have our charity
If, conscious of his guilt, he doth repent.
But he who sees no wrong in what he does —
In arrogant esteem admits no blame —
Thereby alone our charity should lose,
And be no whit entitled to the same!

[46]

Perchance you answer that he cannot see;
But most can see if but they only would,
And those that won't must of our charity
Be thus deprivèd for the common good.
Thus, and thus only, can they ever be
Convinced at last of their iniquity!
Thus only are their eyes restored to sight
Wherewith to recognize their neighbor's right!
However lofty, worthy of esteem,
A noble, gen'rous principle may seem,
We can but weaken — can but dull its gleam —
By carrying to unreasoning extreme.
Even religion can become obsessed
So with itself that it doth lose the best
Of its true message to the hungry soul,
Developing emotion — not control!
The reeling drunkard, quite bereft of wit,
With nerves and senses dulled, submerged in drink,
Less base would seem than thus our souls per-
    mit
In such emotional debauch to sink!
The one but bids a passing, brief farewell
To these, his senses purely physical;
But he, the other, would his reason sell,
Renouncing something intellectual!
Thus even Charity should be controlled,
And we this greatest gift should quite withhold
From those whose selfishness 'twould but pervert,
And give to those for whom 'tis just desert!
Within each soul the secret is supplied
To this, the constant, never failing guide

Which whispers: " Charity should be applied
Only where reasoning conscience doth provide
The answer, which can always be relied
Upon to teach us truly to decide!"

FAITH

" Faith is the intuitive conviction of that which both reason and conscience approve."—*School of Natural Science.*

SOME words are hard exactly to define —
Make unambiguous and plain to see,
And their true meaning rigidly confine
Within the limits of authority.
Such words to many men appear unlike;
To many shades of meaning they relate,
With the result that, when we use them, we
Each other's thoughts but dimly 'proximate.

And one of these — that thing we know as
    " Faith "—
Of many shades of meaning has no dearth;
As many shades, indeed, as tongues to speak,
As ears to hear, or brains to give it birth!
Would not this little word so often used,
So oft applied, misquoted and abused,
Gain value if from all the tongues it came,
As to receiving ears, it meant the same?
To some men faith would seem to be a state
Of mind where Nature's laws we must defy,
And these to no experience relate,
And thus the human brain to stultify!
Were not these minds provided us to use,
And to develop under Nature's plan?
And if we fail, do not we but abuse
The greatest gift of Nature unto Man?
For why should we thus prostitute the mind,

And to the question give a ready " Aye! "
When " No! " is but the answer that we find —
When, as we do, we know that we but lie?
Therefore I say a faith that doth resist
The promptings of our reason and insist
Upon that which the mind can never lend,
Is faith debasèd to an evil end!
Has not unreasoning faith produced a type
Who " faith " indeed — if so it be — have won
By keeping mind from e'er becoming ripe,
Preventing thought from dwelling thereupon?
But what the value of such faith as this,
Which, to believe, must never dare to think,
The which to do but opens an abyss
At which the doubter trembles on the brink?
Not Faith, but Superstition, this, indeed!
Full brother to an old Dogmatic Creed
By Ignorance begot!   The legacy
Of Crude Tradition to posterity!

But there is faith of quite another sort;
A faith in which we can uplift our eyes;
Which needs not that our reason we distort;
A gift, 'bove others, which we most should prize!
It is a gift untinged with abject fear —
No bastard child of pure Malignity —
But something reasonable, plain and clear,
That raises Man to a new dignity!
" *Faith is conviction, clear, intuitive,*
Of that which reasoning conscience doth ap-
     prove! "

No thing of utter unbelief, towards which
Unreasoning emotion would us move!
Such faith as this gives dignity to life;
New strength and courage to the soul of man;
New hope; new effort in the constant strife
To live in sympathy with Nature's plan.
And thus the gifts of Nature do we use,
Respect, conserve, develop — not abuse!
Thus we the Master's talent do employ,
And thereby gain resulting peace and joy!

MORALITY

" Morality is the established harmonic relation which man, as an individual intelligence, sustains to the constructive principle of nature."— *School of Natural Science.*

COULD any other definition give,
More truly than the one above displayed,
The soul, the essence and the inner truth
Of that thing which we call " Morality "?
Is't not, indeed, a meaning that appeals
To all, whate'er their state of life may be,
Whate'er may be their true development
Of mind, of soul, of spirit and of thought?
This does not lay down hard and rigid rules;
Enact those laws which bear unjustly on
Either the one whose slow development
Forever keeps him plodding in the rear,
Or yet on him, that far developed man,
Whose place is always in the foremost van
Of this, the army of humanity.
'Tis fit for him who leads and him who lags,
As well as for that far, far greater force
Which slowly, often painfully, but drags
Its rule-bound life o'er this allotted course.
This meaning tells us not of written laws
By man enacted — laws that can but bear
More heavily on some than others if
They be but suited to the average.
It whispers nothing of tradition's sway,
Nor guides the modern by the ancient way,
Telling that this, or that, decree should last

Because 'twas formulated in the past.
Nor does it indicate those other laws —
Those strange, unwritten, silent laws that we
Impose upon our neighbors and ourselves —
Those laws of pure conventionality.
Nor yet it speaks of those laws called divine —
Those laws which on Mt. Sinai's slopes were
    given
To those rude people who themselves opined
The only chosen of the God of heaven.
The only law it tells of is that law
Which whispers in the conscious soul of Man
And guides his every action by its urge
Towards this the single and eternal plan
Laid down by the Supreme Intelligence.
For every soul has that within itself
By which it is enabled clear to see
When discord reigns within, or when, instead,
All is consistent with true harmony.
An instinct 'tis that we cannot define —
Cannot explain, or prove by rule or line —
But still 'tis there, beyond our will's control,
A primal instinct of the living soul!
An instinct, this, quite individual —
Not subject to coercion or to sway,
E'en by ourselves — but one which ever points
With true precision to the proper way.
For Man himself must be the final judge
Of thought and act which, outwardly concealed,
Are ever 'fore his Consciousness arraigned,
And his most inmost impulse here revealed!

It matters not how much he would excuse,
Or higher motive to his act ascribe,
Such case before this court he'll ever lose —
This court above both sophistry and bribe!
Does not this definition give to Man
A reasoning purpose in the mighty plan,
Conferring 'pon him a new dignity,
And on his soul a fuller sovereignty?
And as he ever has this inner guide
Which harmony and discord thus defines,
So has he also that within which tells
When these, his acts, are on constructive lines.
Destruction spells but discord — never less!
This truth we might as well at once confess;
And true construction must forever be
In full accord with all true harmony;
For Nature is in all harmonious,
And harmony the essence of her sway;
From which it follows that construction must
But represent at last true Nature's way!
'Tis marvelous how Nature thus has set,
Deep down within the soul of every man,
This secret answer to her purposes,
This little key to her eternal plan!
For as the iron to the magnet points —
As points the compass to the distant pole —
To Nature's plan, true and unerringly,
Forever points the compass of the soul!

SCIENCE

"Science is exact knowlede of the facts of nature, classified and systematized."—*School of Natural Science.*

WITHIN this little word there is contained
Much of the sum of knowledge and of truth
Which by Man so laboriously has been
Extracted from the bulk of Nature's store.
How much it seems when we look back upon
The first beginnings of the early man
And note how vastly it has waxed and grown
Within the recent, pure historic span!
And yet how little 'tis if but compared
With those the secrets Nature holds in store
For those whose mind and thought are so pre-
      pared
To wrest from out her bosom more and more!
'Tis like the petty pilferings of a child —
A trifling little sum, a thing of dearth —
Which 'mounts to nothing, when 'tis all compiled,
Compared with all the riches of the earth!
And e'en as children, arrogant and proud
Of these, their little hoardings, Man would seem
At times to feel that he has learned it all,
And from all knowledge skimmed the very cream!
For often, blinded by his present gain,
In self-sufficiency, cannot abstain
From bold assertion, with much pomp and show,
That he, in fact, knows all there is to know;
For when he dubs a thing " Unknowable "
And others' efforts thereby would restrain,

[55]

What is it but an intimation that
All knowledge is contained within his brain?
Else wherefore should he thus profess to speak
About another — or about that field
Wherein he works — when others also seek
What, lost to him, to them may be revealed?
'Tis but a petty arrogance of thought
That thus 'pon other thought would put a ban;
Desire alone to teach — not to be taught —
An indication of the child in Man!
And others, with more self-conceit than they,
While ridiculing this, their neighbor's cause,
Would their own suppositions e'en portray
As representing truly Nature's laws!
While delving in the field of Nature, they
May chance upon a little grain of truth
As yet unfound, wherewith they would, forsooth,
Erect an edifice sublime, profound,
But without width of base or depth of ground.
Thus are these towering structures often built
Of suppositions, bold, unique and grand,
Which fain would tower to Heaven, but which
    can't
Because they have foundations on the sand!
For Science is alone concerned with facts;
And knowledge, not hypothesis, its due;
And thus these towering edifices fall
If these foundations prove at last untrue!
How well if those of scientific bent
Would with their own true field but be content,
And in the chain of knowledge forge their link

While granting others equal right to think!
The chain, indeed, is great enough; and ought
Not knowledge found inspire the knowledge
  sought?
For fact ne'er yet did fact annihilate,
But further search for fact but stimulate.
That seeming fact which other fact would prove
A thing untrue, 'twere better we remove
From out our consciousness and build again
Some other structure that will bear the strain.
True Science has no place — far less a need —
For superstition, dogma, or for creed,
Its own or others', or should cherish ruth
For that which crumbles 'neath the light of Truth.
And if its own delusions it would spurn
As quick as now on others' it would turn,
How much of wastage could be cleared away
That now obstructs the shining light of day!
For thoughts outgrown are thoughts we should
  remove,
Lest their continued presence do but prove
An obstacle to fuller thought, forsooth —
A thought more pregnant with the vital truth.
And we must fully realize that we
Cannot dictate what can, and cannot, be;
Cannot, indeed, erect a fence as though
To say: "Beyond this Man can never go"!
When we our false hypotheses discard
And our small store of knowledge but discern,
Nor let the word "Unknowable" retard,
Then — not till then — will we be ripe to learn.

When all these childish traits we have outgrown,
How much now "Unknown" will become the
    "Known"!
With what a crop the field of Nature sown!
How vast, indeed, the future prospect shown!

TRUTH

"Truth is the established relation which the facts of Nature sustain to each other and to the individual intelligence or soul of man."—*School of Natural Science.*

How small a word is this, indeed, to hold
A thing so vital to the soul of Man!
How frail a compass wherein to incase
The inner essence of all Nature's plan!
But Truth is often paradoxical,
And often true that which appears absurd;
Therefore why marvel at the height and depth
Of greatness held within this little word?
Nor should we marvel if, indeed, at times
Its fuller meaning should escape our clutch,
When we consider that five letters form
The small receptacle that holds so much!
For some this little word would greatly stretch
Far, far beyond its meaning and its due,
And thus make of it but a cloak with which
To cover much that is, indeed, untrue;
For Truth to some is as they, only, see —
Not that which is, but what they think should be,
And to such people 'tis a great surprise
That all the world cannot see through their eyes!
But is the vision of the worm as true
As of the eagle, soaring in the blue?
Can light-blind bat that in the sunlight blinks
Compare his orb with the far-seeing lynx?
And even so it is the case with Man,
For some cannot perceive what others can;

And some, indeed, deny that that can be
Which to a truer sight is plain to see.
But here, within the kingdom of the Man,
The field is broader far and hard to scan,
For to his vision purely physical
Are added others intellectual;
And 'pon them all a moral field imposed —
A field to which some human eyes are closed!
Thus if we find such great disparity
Within a kingdom of a single field,
Would not it seem, indeed, a rarity
If different eyes the same result revealed
In this, a region where much is concealed?
For here the sight is not of things so plain —
Of things that we may touch, or taste, or smell —
But of those visions of the heart and soul
Whereon the mind of Man alone may dwell!
And as one eye, from other eye distinct,
Can see but part while other views the whole,
So is it with the impulse of the heart,
As with the intuition of the soul.
But as, with varying strength of vision, we
Exert, or lag, or reason, or but guess,
The Truth stands ever constant, strong and free,
For Truth is Truth — no more, and never less!
Thus Truth is like a rock, set in the deep,
Round which the forces of our nature sweep;
At times 'tis lost to view midst mists of doubt;
Again, at other times, quite blotted out
By waves of anger, or by sleets of fear;
But, these once passed, again it doth appear

Erect, upstanding, definite and clear!
For what is Truth but the establishèd
Relation which the facts of Nature bear
Unto each other and unto the soul —
The individual intelligence —
Of this the creature that we know as Man?
If that we fail to glimpse its massive form —
Its great, majestic lines, so stern and bare —
We can but charge our blindness to the storm
Of passing doubt, for Truth is ever there
Unchanged and changeless in the lapse of Time —
A wondrous shape, majestic, pure, sublime;
A thing outliving present, future, past;
A form that shall endure while Time shall last!

PHILOSOPHY

" Philosophy is the conclusions which men, in their search for a knowledge of truth, have drawn from the facts of Science."— *School of Natural Science.*

FAR back within the dim and distant past,
When consciousness of self did first arise,
The early man, but little 'bove the brute,
Did make weak efforts to philosophize.
For Nature's forces must have so impressed
Themselves upon his brain that even then
He must have sought the answer and have tried
To bring her processes within his ken.
But if the human mind, e'en in this day,
To Ignorance so firmly stands enthralled,
To him what must have seemed blind Nature's
    sway
Which so intensely his weak brain appalled?
To him each fact of Nature was a sign —
If good at times, more often still, malign —
Beneath the which he could but cringe and cower
In this the presence of some higher power
Which, though himself to it he must resign,
He still must needs with evil motives dower;
And these same evil spirits must placate —
Their quenchless thirst for blood must ever
    sate —
By sacrificing that he held most dear,
Or else live ever under quivering fear.
Thus had Philosophy its early birth
Among the crude and childish of the earth,

And thus, e'en now, 'tis little more sublime
To those, the thoughtless of the present time!
For many walk in Superstition's way,
And bow e'en yet to her malignant sway,
And live in doubt and dread for fear that they
May fail at times her mandates to obey!
And yet how many would their acts relate
To that obscure, that prehistoric state
To which they are, indeed, so closely bound —
Which naught but Reason can at all abate?
But in the mind of Man so much doth grow
That Reason's growth is stunted, weak and slow,
And he but dull to see that, freed from tares,
It, of them all, the richest harvest bears!
And so the growth of this Philosophy,
This child of Reason, ever must keep pace
With this, the slow march of humanity —
The ever constant progress of the race.
But in all ages there has ever been
The little handful — they, the thinking men
Who have outstripped their fellows and have seen
That which was not within their neighbors' ken.
And they the leaven are that leavens all —
That break the shackles of their brothers' thrall,
That ever point the way to Truth and Right
And show that Knowledge is the road to Might!
But as Philosophy is but, indeed,
Conclusions which men draw — while in the search
For this, the knowledge of the very Truth —
From these, the facts of Science and of life,
How happens it that, in the distant past,

[63]

When Science was as yet a thing unborn,
So much of Truth was caught and still held fast
That later Science proves was nobly won?
Must not they, lacking Science, have been led
By Intuition to the fountain-head
Of this, the spring of Truth, which ever flows —
E'en before Reason out of darkness rose?
But now, with Science as our constant guide,
What cause remains in darkness to abide?
And with the light by Intuition brought,
Is not all life with wondrous beauty fraught
And pregnant with such possibilities
As we as yet can dimly but surmise?
Thus if Philosophy in ages gone,
While but the child of Intuition born,
Could thus give birth to e'en one living truth,
What multitude of progeny, forsooth,
Should from the loins of both of them be drawn!
And not in number merely, but in strength
Of vital force and life, until at length
The chains of bondage from our limbs it rives
And gives a greater freedom to our lives!
Nor will we e'er regret the thing that's gone,
For true Philosophy will then adorn
Our lives — Philosophy by Science won,
Of Reason and of Intuition born!

RELIGION

"Religion is the application of the facts of Science and the conclusions of Philosophy to individual life and conduct."—*School of Natural Science.*

How strange this definition must appear
To those who, trained in other ways of thought,
Have, in the distant past rather than here,
The inner meaning of Religion sought!
For they have e'er insisted that belief
Must first of all be unbelievable,
And thereby must they ever come to grief
In matters that are controvertible!
And is not this belief of theirs — if we
May so describe a thing that bears no part
Of true belief — but blind attempt to see
And read the hidden impulse of the heart?
For in the effort they have borrowed much
Of pagan ritual and pagan rite,
And used base superstition as a clutch
To grasp, to hold, suppress and to affright.
And thus they have purloined the Virgin Birth,
The Resurrection; and have sought to cast
These outgrown fallacies o'er all the earth —
These superstitions of a distant past!
And even this, their Holy Sacrament —
That Eucharist of theirs that would assuage
The sins of Man — what is it but a strange
And atavistic relapse to an age
So crude and brutal, so devoid of light,
That Man would deify and would endower

[65]

His fellow with divinity and might,
Then slay and eat — thus to obtain his power?
If but the page of history we scan,
We find that ever the outstanding man —
He who would bring a message to the earth —
Was thus announced as of a virgin birth!
What strange perversity to thus insist
Immaculate conception such as this
Can lend an honor or a dignity,
Or be aught else than pure malignity
Attacking thus Man's reason and, indeed,
Debasing him to some crude pagan creed!
But much of savage lingers in him still,
Which shackles mind and thought and soul and
    will,
And prompts him to accept and to believe
That which his reasoning mind cannot conceive!
Full many things, indeed, in heaven and earth
Undreamed of are in our philosophy,
But should this prompt us to permit the birth,
Unchecked, of all perverted sophistry?
In this enlightened age is not, indeed,
This pagan worship an anachronism —
This blind adherence to dogmatic creed,
A crude and stultifying solecism?
And does not worship of Tradition's word,
Which reasoning conscience doth pronounce ab-
    surd,
Make light of knowledge, ignorance retain,
And stamp its lasting impress on the brain?
Religion such as this has served its time,

Its cause and purpose in the years gone by,
And 'bove it now the present age would climb
And place its visions and conceptions high
'Bove such a crude, anthropomorphic god!
And why should not Religion lead the fight —
Take its true station in the foremost van —
Not hamper, but inspire — enlarge the sight,
And strike the shackles from the soul of Man?
But old dogmatic Creed is ever blind,
And so self-centred that it thinks to bind,
By antiquated methods such as these,
The living and enquiring human mind!
It cannot see that progress must progress!
Confessing others, it will not confess!
Thus blind conservatism is its goal —
An end to paltry for the living soul.
Its every action is reactionary;
Itself the arbiter — is arbitrary;
And thus its edicts launches but to find
No answering impulse in the growing mind!
If from its present stand 'twill not diverge,
Advancing human thought will soon submerge,
O'erwhelm, engulf and utterly destroy
Their grain of Truth mixed with so much alloy!
By these is meant that far, far greater force
That still pursues the same unyielding course
As in the past, ere Man had come to see
That all was not as they professed must be.
But there are others, few in number, who
Direct his eyes to a far fairer view;
Who would, to mind and soul, grant full franchise

And point the way to truer paradise.
They teach him that Religion is no thing
Of creed and dogma, recompense or sting,
For this belief or that, or bid him turn
And take to heart that which his mind would
    spurn.
They show him that Religion is, indeed,
Naught but conclusions of Philosophy
And application of the facts of Science
To this, his own and individual life;
The which to do he must accept the facts,
Absorb, digest, and reproduce in acts
Conforming with the purpose and the plan
Harmonious Nature has laid down for Man.
Thus — and thus only — can he ever be
A true collaborator in the work
The which to do at last will set him free,
But which he can, if so he wills, but shirk!
And to the task Nature would have him bring
Each shred of intuition, reason, mind,
And all at once into the balance fling,
That by this conscious effort he may find
The inner secret to her purposes!
'Tis not by blinding eyes we strive to see!
'Tis not by stopping ears we best can hear!
'Tis not by shutting mind we learn to be
A being self-controlled, devoid of fear!
Nor is it by renouncing this, our right,
And placing in some other hands our hope —
Be he archbishop, cardinal, or pope —
That these, our eyes, are opened to the light!

For this is but to prostitute the mind,
And it to other mind to pay as fee —
An act more base, ignoble, I do find,
Than body prostitution e'er could be!
Each for himself the riddle has to solve,
And each from low to higher life evolve;
Thus, self-controlled the mind must ever be,
The soul unquestioned in its sovereignty.
And this should be our ever-constant goal:
To be, alone, the master of the soul,
The mind and body, too, and subject all
To our own individual control!
If this we do and do apply the facts
Of Science and of true Philosophy
To this, our conduct and our daily lives,
We need not question if the patient thrives;
For thought, indeed, begets but higher thought
And light will come to those who light have
     sought —
Transforming darkness into brightest day —
If they but seek it in the proper way!
And will not then Religion come to be
The guide that first the mind and soul would free,
Then points to Man the proper course that he,
Commencing here, keeps through Eternity?

THOUGHT

How marvelous and grand, the power of Thought!
With what tremendous attributes 'tis fraught!
How great the possibilities that lie
There hidden, if but diligently sought!

'Tis like an unexplored and hidden mine,
Whose limitations no one can define,
That yields rich ore to all who dig, and which,
In being worked, doth but itself refine!

For Thought develops Thought, and in this wise,
Low Thought to higher Thought must ever rise,
With nothing that can check its growth, indeed,
Beneath the vast, illimitable skies!

This, then, the prospect for the man who works
This property of his!   But he who shirks
The labor may at last but come to find
A latent evil force that therein lurks!

For he who works not, does the trust betray,
And Thought untrained is Thought but led
    astray;
And what doth not advance, cannot stand still,
But sinks to desolation and decay!

'Twould seem that Nature hath provided so
That back or forward everything must go —
That Mutability, alone unchanged,
Must, like a pendulum, swing to and fro!

'Tis ever thus in Nature and in Man!
Progress or retrogression is the ban
That Nature places 'pon all things that live —
This her eternal, unexcepting plan.

For thus, and only thus indeed, she may
Impress upon our intellects her sway,
And thus through evolution indicate
To our weak senses this, her only way!

And so we sense the law of proper use —
Dimly, 'tis true, for still our grasp is loose
'Pon this conception; and we still must play
With that, our own — the man-made law, abuse!

For all she gives us, we must rightly use,
Though having power, indeed, but to abuse;
The choice is ours, and Nature leaves us free —
Submits them both, and then would have us
    choose.

Thus Thought is subject to development —
Or retrogression, if that be our bent;
And both the goals are plain and clear to see —
Content, the one; the other, discontent!

But if development be this, our aim —
By which is meant not wealth, nor power, nor
    fame,
But true development of mind and thought —
How strangely fascinating is the game!

For Thought is pregnant with a mighty force,
And unimpeded doth pursue its course,
Nor lags, nor wavers, for it draws supply
From the exhaustless, fundamental source!

What other power compares with this alone?
If owned, should we not other loss condone?
For, with all else, if this we lack, what can
For this, the greatest loss of all, atone?

Thus Thought, and Thought alone, conditions life,
Produces harmony; engenders strife;
Gives weight and substance to all things that be —
Both good and bad, exceptional or rife!

And Thought, when clothed in words, when winged
        with speech,
Encircles Space, and out of Time doth reach
From distant past to ages yet unborn,
The never-dying word of Thought to teach!

For Thought is ever new — untouched by rust —
And still within our consciousness would thrust
Some gem of Thought conceivèd in a brain
For many centuries returned to dust!

Thus Thought lives on, e'en when the mother womb
That gave it birth has vanished in the tomb!
Perpetual life that never fades or dies!
Unfailing flower of true perennial bloom!

How great a blessing if we would but lay
These flowers of Thought within our minds today,
Would sow the seeds and cultivate them well,
And reap at last the harvest that we may!

LIFE'S JOURNEY

Life seems to me but as a journey made
From the rose-tinted, eastern peak of Birth,
Down through the valley lying in between,
And up the farther, rocky, western slope
To that, the dreary, darkling crest of Death!
A journey which, begun in morning glow
And fanned by early zephyrs light and sweet,
Becomes at length, in torrid pain below,
A battle with the cruel and stifling heat,
At last becoming — on the farther slope,
When evening shadows have begun to fall —
A dim and misty path whereon to grope
And fight for strength 'gainst visions that appal
The mind and heart devoid of faith and hope,
The which, if lost, we rarely can recall.

Through infancy and childhood's happy years,
Through childish joys and sorrows, hopes and
    fears —
Those passing clouds upon a summer sky
That only wash it brighter with their tears —
Awhile doth childhood dawdle on the crest,
Bathed in the first soft light of early dawn;
Viewing alone the present with full zest
And heedless of those voices that would warn;
Assuming life a merriment and jest,
And those who caution but as strange, depressed
Weaklings from whom all strength of life is gone;
Until, grown strong at last, its eyes are drawn

To those far peaks, now bathed in glowing morn,
When eagerly it enters on its quest.
Heedless and merry doth the trip begin;
And life seems like some rich and boundless store
With naught to lose but everything to win,
And winning e'er increasing more and more.
Thus with a deprecating air, disdainful toss,
Impatiently he hears, indeed, that loss
Perchance may meet him on the way ahead —
Loss, pain, despondency, despair and dread!

At first the slope is easy, free from care —
Sun-kissed the vision, tonic-like the air,
And flowering shrubs and vines but lend their
    touch
To make still fairer life that is so fair.
Gay butterflies swing lightly to the breeze,
Charming the eye and tempting hand to seize
And foot to stray from out the forward path,
If only pent up spirit to release.
And 'pon each bough, with all their might and
    main,
Full-throated songsters warble their refrain,
Each note of which inspires but joy and hope
Of all that waits him on the farther slope.
He finds new fruits, before unknown, to taste;
New feelings, new sensations, yet untried,
O'er which he often pressing time doth waste
Without a thought of what they may betide,
For youth must learn from sad experience,
Without the which it never can be sure,

And this must be its final recompense
For all that it has cost it to secure.

And now he is convinced that he who warned
Was but some spectre shape at this, life's spread —
A being to be pitied more than scorned,
Some crude and croaking phantom of the dead,
Some human wreckage cast upon the shore
Of this, life's joyous, full and flowing tide,
One who, perchance, had lived, but lived no more
And who, though breathing, otherwise had died!
And so adown the eastern slope he goes,
With eyes strained forward to that later strife
In which he sees but conquest — never woes —
Conquest of all attainable in life.
Courage pervades his heart and hope his eye;
His strength with other strength he longs to try;
And thus inspired, beneath the morning sun
He dreams alone of glories to be won.
And life, to him, is but a pleasing game —
The road to full attainment, wealth and fame;
And all its paths are but for him to choose,
For of them all the end would seem the same —
The same, at least, to those of spirit, force;
To those who recognize, like him, the course,
And for all others he has but disdain,
The which to show he hardly can refrain.
Thus gaily he traverses this, the first,
Stage of his journey, with no thought or dread
Of weariness, of hunger, or of thirst
That may await him on the path ahead.

But soon the downward slope is left behind
And the rough valley stretches at his feet,
And then alone there flashes through his mind
The thought of coming hardships he must meet.
But courage fails him not and he is strong —
Weak in experience, but strong in hope,
The which sustains him though the way seem long
And unknown dangers 'fore his vision ope'.
But now rough boulders rise within his path,
And turbid currents interrupt the way,
And tangling vines his footsteps oft impede,
Or treacherous morass his feet betray.
The scorching sunlight now doth blind his eyes,
Beating 'pon unprotected head and brow,
While ever in his path new objects rise,
Which strive to interfere, deter, or cow.
New difficulties to be overcome,
New problems he must wrestle with and solve,
An ever-growing load — a lengthening sum
Demanding all his strength and firm resolve.
But now experience comes to his aid
And teaches how he may at times evade,
Escape, or pass some pitfalls into which
His former lack of it had made him pitch.
But some, while gaining this experience
For which they needs must ever blindly grope,
Cast quite aside, or utterly forget,
Their former compass — that of faith and hope.
But he is wise who doth retain it still,
And often at its fountain drink his fill,
For it provides a cordial the which

Experience alone cannot distil.
Experience may save him many a fall,
Many a needless suffering and pain,
But faith and hope provide the wherewithal
To transmute seeming loss into a gain;
And it alone provides that inner strength
That gladdens heart and lights despondent eyes
And gives conviction to the soul at length
That good from evil will at last arise!
But those who in their haste have thrown away
This guiding compass which to youth is given,
Find little solace in the burning day
And learn that much of strength from life is riven.
For mere experience, while of great need,
Has limitations, and at times, indeed,
But hardens and destroys that inner sight
The which enables us to see the light!
Thus through the valley he pursues his way,
His eyes firm-set upon the farther slope,
While many faint and fall, digress or stray,
Without the guiding light of faith and hope.

At last the valley's crossed, and here, at length,
In the cool shadows of the lengthening day,
He pauses to renew his failing strength
Ere turning once again unto the way.
After the scorching sunlight of the plain,
The rocky path, the treacherous morass,
The cooling shadow tempts him and he fain
Would now postpone the passage of the pass
That frowns above with many a beetling crag,

Suggesting dangers that his thoughts harass.
But on this journey none may ever lag,
And though he fain would rest, he still must drag
His aching limbs and summon all his will
To tread the path stretching before him still.
And here, within the afternoon of life,
E'en more than in the burning heat of day
When mind and heart were occupied with strife,
He'll need his compass lest he lose his way;
For if his ideals have been left behind,
Or lost, or shattered in the noon-day strain,
What guide remains for this, his active mind —
What answers to the questions of his brain?
Experience but whispers of the past,
Of all that's gone before it is the sum;
But what strong guiding light can it now cast
Upon those other dangers yet to come?
For at this stage, intuitively, he
Begins — if dimly, still, indeed — to see
That out ahead the way is not the same
As that familiar one by which he came;
And though the latter was both rough and rude,
The present effort all his fancies wooed
And tempted him to banish from his mind
Those other thoughts that would at times ob-
    trude.
But now they can no longer be escaped
Here in the gathering dusk of early eve,
And he must meet them as his mind is shaped
To weigh, to measure, reject, or receive.
With what equipment he has forged within —

Be it of simple fool, or learned sage —
He now must gird himself and must begin
Of this, his trip, the last and final stage.
And lucky he with ideals unimpaired;
With soul responsive; spirit firm and strong;
With mental vision clear, and mind prepared
To see, to gauge, to measure right and wrong!
For now the way is tortuous and steep,
And evening shadows stealthily do creep
Upon his path and make dim and obscure
That which at first had seemed so plain and sure.
And evening mists rise in the hollow spots,
Converting but to nebulous grey blots
Secluded dells which early morning light
Had made to seem so wondrous fair and bright.
And often sheets of cold and driving rain —
Now dreary drizzle, now torrential flood —
But add their part to his increasing pain,
And chill still faster his fast chilling blood.
And now he stumbles where before he leapt;
The way, once bounded, must at last be crept
Painfully slow, to husband failing strength,
If he would measure the full journey's length.
And as he creeps, the ever-growing chill
Clutches his heart and stifles mind and will,
And the exultant harmony of morn
Seems, in life's evening, desolate and still.

Thus plods the man of faith and hope bereft —
He whose ideals, shattered in the fight,
Finds at the last that he, indeed, has left

His consolation 'gainst the coming night!
For here experience hath naught to say
Save of his journey in the vanished day
That's past and gone, and has no word of cheer
To help dispel that chilling breath of fear
Of which he has become the living prey
Now that the crest of Death appears so near.
But he, the man whose faith and hope are strong,
Ne'er wavers now, but rather with a song
Upon his lips the journey's end doth greet,
Nor would, indeed, continuance prolong.
For with the eye of faith he plainly sees
That which the other does by slow degrees,
And intuition clearly points the way
To a continuous and brighter day —
A day which, starting at the crest of Death —
From present life divided by a breath —
Continues what was here but just begun,
Granting to each the recompenses won.
His place therein, what he, himself, has made;
The purchase price whereof himself has paid
In thought and act, while on the journey here,
When he, unthinking, the foundations laid.
And if the place be high, or be it low,
There to his own place he of needs must go
And reap the harvest to be gathered there,
The seed whereof in this life he did sow;
For Nature is unswerving, true and just —
Undeviating and alike to all —
E'en as the force of gravitation must
The up-thrown stone reverse unto a fall.

No matter what his thought or best belief!
If true, 'tis well! If not, 'twill come to grief
When at the last the inner truth stands forth
And that WHICH IS appears in bold relief!
If in his act or thought he's led astray
By those professing here to know the way,
He need not these, his fellows, then abuse
Because he failed his intellect to use;
For each is in himself endowed with mind —
That wondrous thing with latent vigor fraught —
Wherewith to search, and Nature's secrets find.
The which he may, if diligently sought.
Nor need he look for help, indeed, to those
Who sought while here his actions to revise,
For self-appointed stewardship shall close
When death shall close those same judicial eyes.
Then will he see the journey here has been
But Nature's method — Nature's single way —
Of granting him permission thus to sin,
Demanding in return that he must pay.
And sin — no thing of fixed and standard rule;
No precept taught in court-house, church or
    school;
A thing to master, like a lengthy sum
By memory — the gift of sage and fool!
For sin, indeed, quite otherwise would seem —
A thing more weighty, pregnant with a cause —
And comes at last to be all that we deem
A contravention of true Nature's laws!
And thus the mind must ever judge and weigh —
Must hold or loose, accelerate or stay —

Both thought and act, comparing each and all
With what we deem to be true Nature's way.
And here our reasoning conscience is our guide —
That spirit shape untrammelled, full and free,
Which, if consulted, helps us to decide
Truly between what should, and should not, be.
Thus ever is the choice 'twixt good and ill;
And we — free agents — have the power to
    choose;
But obligation also, if we lose,
To meet the score with prompt and ready will.
And grudging penury at this, the debt,
Will not one whit the reckoning offset,
But rather add an interest charge which we
At time of settlement may well regret!
Thus is life's journey but a training school.
In which the rudiments of life are taught,
And where, if dimly, we perceive the rule
With which, indeed, all future life is fraught!
And if we're indolent and slow to learn —
In petty pride, refuse what's in our reach —
Pain comes to warn us that we must not spurn
The lessons Nature is prepared to teach.
How, other, could we learn than in this way,
Within the compass of a fleeting day?
How, otherwise, is character derived
If not by something, seemingly deprived,
That moves to thought and action, lacking which,
Means to the end had never been contrived?
Would any strive for that which they ne'er
    need?

[83]

Why sow at all but for the harvest seed
That doth repay the effort o'er and o'er —
No matter what the field, or who the sower?
Thus, constantly doth Nature spur us on
By holding 'fore us prizes to be won;
And thus doth Nature cause us to refrain
By the infliction of the thing called Pain!

These are the lessons which our faith and hope —
In all their marvelous, far-reaching scope —
Bring to our senses if we are prepared
With ears to hear and eyes, indeed, to ope.
And this the vital truth the traveler sees
While toiling up the drear and rugged slope;
And, seeing this, he knows his present pain
Is but disguisèd benefit and gain
If understood, as useless ore, when mined,
Becomes of use when properly refined.
As every product of the teeming earth
Can be converted to a thing of worth,
So all his ills, destructive though they be,
Can be, indeed, applied constructively.
And thus misfortune can be made a boon —
A store of riches, growing more and more,
And coming to fulfillment, late or soon,
If we from out the husk extract the core.
Thus seeing, with a song within his heart,
The man of faith and hope pursues his way,
Undauntedly performing this, his part,
In full conviction of the coming day!
This is his faith that nothing can dispel!

This is his courage that no force can quell!
No recompense of heaven, nor threat of hell,
But what his reasoning conscience doth compel —
Saying at last: " 'Tis done, and it is well!"

THE MIND OF CHILDHOOD

THE mind of childhood, like a budding flower,
Unfolds its form of beauty hour by hour,
And daily doth expand, increase and grow
As added knowledge doth with graces dower!
At first, while in the bud shut close and still,
But few impressions make its senses thrill
And it lies dormant in the morn of life,
Heedless, unthinking, gaining strength, until
It blossoms forth, at last, in thought and will!
And then its appetite is strong and keen —
Sharp and enquiring as a cutting knife —
And straightway it begins to reap and glean
All grain of knowledge in the field of life.
Wheat grains of truth — life-giving, pure and
     strong —
But also weeds of untruth, tares of wrong,
And briars and thistles of perverted thought
Seem to it, all alike, with value fraught!
Full often are these weeds and tares possessed
Of greater charm, in fuller beauty dressed,
Alluring to the eyes that on them dwell,
More fascinating to the taste and smell!
Seductive vices, gayest colors show;
Perverted thought in beauteous form doth blow;
Revealing not their poisonous quality,
Unreasoning superstitions often grow!
Midst such a crop, how can childhood decide
Without a wise and understanding guide
To show, to reason — never to command;

A leading, guiding — not a driving — hand?
A hand that clearly, calmly, points the way,
Lest trusting childhood should itself betray,
And, by the reaping of the tares and weeds,
For later fatal harvest glean the seeds!
And sympathetic, understanding, wise
Must be the mind that childhood would apprize
Of all these things, and would attempt to guide
Its ready brain and wide, enquiring eyes!
For childhood's mind is as a spotless page,
Untouched, unsullied by the hand of age,
Unwarped by strain, unprejudiced by strife —
Childhood's, as yet, unspotted page of life!
As black shows blackest 'gainst the driven snow,
So 'pon this page all stains will darkest show;
Or as a seed, planted in virgin soil,
To fuller, ripe luxuriance will grow!
So with the mind of childhood each impress,
At first so strong, grows ever less and less
And faint and fainter with the passing years,
As mind grows callous with its doubts and fears.
Therefore upon this spotless page of youth,
Which takes impressions as 'twill later not,
Should not we strive but to impress the truth,
Nor mar its tender surface with a blot?
No blot of Superstition, rank and rude —
The bastard offspring of perverted Thought —
Should be permitted 'pon it to obtrude,
And leave its stain upon its surface wrought.
How oft, in thoughtless folly, do we cast
Some outgrown superstition of the past

'Pon childhood's trusting mind, creating there
A crude encumbrance — useless first and last!
How often do we generate a fear
Which leaves its imprint, desolate and drear,
And, grown to strength from this initial seed,
In after life conditions thought and deed!
For, with imagination full and free,
Emotion warm, pulsating — neither led
By reason, cold and clear — how can it see
That here, indeed, is little cause for dread?
For superstition, crude, perverted, blind,
Finds scanty lodgment in the virile mind
That's grown to full maturity and strength
Unless in youth it be allowed to bind.
And blind, unthinking fear — indeed the worst
Of all the ills with which this life is cursed —
Is easy to implant in childish thought
If by — what seems to it — true wisdom taught!
For fear is but alone a thing of use
To point the consequences of abuse
Of Nature's laws, and should be made to be
A tool with which to work constructively.
And fear that has no cause 'gainst which to guard
Can never strengthen, but must e'er retard
The growth of mind and reason, bringing pain
That's loss complete, without a shred of gain.
And childhood has, at best, enough to fear;
Enough to learn; enough to understand;
Without impressing 'pon it such a drear
And nameless terror of a hidden hand.
For living is replete enough with strife,

And with full many things which we must dread,
Without implanting thus within our life
Some out-lived superstition of the dead!
And we can ne'er be greater than we think!
And if our aim be thought serene and high,
We miss the mark — to lower level sink —
If under Superstition's hand we lie.
'Tis bad enough to so misuse our own —
For which, no doubt, we shall in full atone —
But criminal indeed if thus we bind
With such a load, the trusting childish mind!
How little wisdom hath maturity
That thus would bind where it should strive to
    free!
How strange an office for the loving heart,
Not help, but actual hindrance, to impart;
To foster weakness — not to further strength —
In one beloved, which will indeed, at length,
By dulling reason, clouding mind and brain,
Make him less fit to stand life's heavy strain!
The opening bud of childhood we should nurse
With greater wisdom, greater thought and care,
And not attempt to blight it with a curse,
If we expect the blossom to be fair!
If but these cankering evils we remove,
The full-blown bloom itself will surely prove
That this, our tending, has been wise and just —
That we, indeed, have not betrayed the trust!

OLD AGE

SHOULD not Old Age reap from its crop of years
A ceaseless solace, pure perennial balm,
A mind devoid alike of doubts and fears,
A spirit high, a soul serene and calm?

Should not a fuller knowledge of the way
Of life and thought make life itself more clear,
And to the mind — as to the heart — convey
A message fraught with comfort, hope and cheer?

Youth's passions o'er, its paroxysms past —
Its mountain torrent, vigorous and free,
Flows deeper far (if not, indeed, so fast)
A-down the level reaches to the sea.

And if the final stretch be cold and bleak,
Should this, in truth, be charged to age alone,
Or to ourselves, thus prompting us to seek
The cause thereof, for which we but atone?

The tree in which the heart and soul have died
While clothed in bloom, turns hard and cold and
    grey,
With rigid branches, leaves close-curled and
    dried —
A spot of desolation by the way.

But it which still the sap of life contains
Sinks ever gently to autumnal rest,

And as a living beauty spot remains
A dash of color upon Nature's breast.

The wealth of varied shade and depth of tone
Vie with the rainbow arching overhead,
And by their beauty indicate alone
The fact that summer days are past and dead.

Why not the same in our autumnal days,
When failing strength and life's less ardent flow
Should purge the dross, and from within us raise
A purer beauty — more celestial glow?

How differs the perspective of the past,
Viewed from the stand-point of our later years!
How vain the stake for which the die oft cast —
The misdirected efforts — useless tears!

And as our eyes a-down the years we strain,
How much we grasp which formerly we spurned —
See past misfortune turned to present gain —
Some lesson mastered, otherwise unlearned!

Is it, indeed, not Mother Nature's plan
To grant a halting place upon the way,
That from its vantage we may closely scan
The thought and impulse of our early day?

For thus the picture-puzzle we call Life
Takes shape and form, a-while we idly dream,
And from afar, unhampered by the strife,
We dimly sense the purpose of the scheme.

And, sensing this, we glimpse the heart and soul
Of life itself, and with redoubled zest
Direct our efforts to the distant goal —
The Golden Fleece — the universal quest.

Thus should Old Age, with doubts and fears sub-
    dued,
Search the untrodden, as the trodden, way,
And, with true courage, faith and hope imbued,
Reflect the coming of a fairer day.

NATURE AFTER RAIN

Did'st ever sit with Nature, after rain,
At sunset, in the springtime of the year,
And list to her harmonious refrain —
That voiceless voice, so subtle yet so clear?

That voice which speaks in every weed and
      flower —
In every leaf, in every blade of grass;
That wondrous anthem so replete with power;
That hushed, but yet reverberating, mass!

Upon each bough the feathered songsters preen
And voice their joy anew, but even they
Serve but to swell that other voice unseen
That takes the major part in Nature's lay.

That strange, impressive harmony of earth —
That voice so low and yet, indeed, so loud —
Insistently proclaiming life and birth,
Changing to swaddling clothes the funeral shroud.

Each grass blade clasps a diamond to its breast;
Each laden bush a bounteous largess throws;
Upon each pendant leaf, in strange unrest,
A living jewel scintillates and glows!

Earth, having drunk a-full the living stream,
Refreshed and thankful, renovated, fair —
Her moistened lips and thirst-quenched voice
      would seem
To ope' and raise in mute and silent prayer.

And all her teeming lives but add their part
To swell the chorus of the joyful strain,
And, voiced or voiceless, speak from out the heart
In this triumphal pæan to the rain!

These myriad voices of the sentient earth
That speak alone of living and rebirth;
Of life, though seeming lost, to be rewon,
E'en though, to our weak senses, past and done!

Can any list' to Nature's song at eve
And still continue but to dread and grieve?
Can any hear and yet with bated breath,
Mutter his doubts and fears of coming death?

Can any fail to see that in the end —
Through all its changes, all its seeming strife —
Life is the goal toward which all things but tend —
That Death must, at the last, give place to Life?

A REFLECTION

Dost ever walk the busy city streets
And contemplate that flowing human tide —
That endless stream that endlessly doth glide,
And which, where'er we turn, the vision greets?

How oft in rapt attention do I gaze
Into the faces that but hurry by,
Each 'pon a mission of its own, and try
To read their thoughts, their purposes, their
    ways!

Active and light; deliberate and slow;
Cheerful and gay; disconsolate and sad;
Depressed, subdued, exuberant and glad —
Appear in this kaleidoscopic show!

Some bent and broken by a lengthy strife;
Some but inspired by all it holds in store —
The cup but sipped, clamor for more and more
Of this intoxicating drink of life!

The cup of life that every one must drink —
So sweet to some; to others naught but gall,
A nauseous dose, a bondage and a thrall
Beneath the which their failing strength doth sink.

And yet to all — where'er their lot be cast —
Is not, indeed, the final goal the same?
Is not the stake in this, life's mighty game,
But that of happiness, from first to last?

But yet, how differently conceived by each!
How varied are the shades it seems to wear!
How many are the trials we must bear
Ere we perceive what Nature has to teach!

How oft our valuations prove untrue!
How highly prized that which, when we attain,
We find contains not happiness, but pain,
And then our time and effort sadly rue!

The disappointed, the disconsolate —
How often are they those but led astray
By some false aim, those fallen in the way
Of clouded reason, mind intemperate? —

They who the fruit of happiness would grasp,
Yet but mistook that which doth it contain
And, having spent themselves and life in vain,
Find naught but dust and ashes in their clasp.

Those who see naught but what appeals to sense;
Those living naught but a material life —
In thought, in aspiration and in strife —
At last receive the proper recompense.

Those who conceive, alone, a selfish goal —
Self-centred souls in bondage unto self,
Seekers of place, of power, of paltry pelf —
In final disappointment pay the toll.

Mistakes of living, commonplace and rife!
Deluded souls who've wandered from the way
And after some strange god have gone astray,
Losing the living verities of life!

How many such as this we daily see!
How few that show conviction and content;
The mind upon some higher ideal bent;
The eye that radiates serenity!

Why is it thus?   And why should it so be?
This disproportion in the human mind
That makes it hard, among the bound, to find
The few in number who seem truly free —

Free from despondency and dread and fear;
From anger, malice, or the lust of gain;
From false ambition, or some form of pain
That renders life but desolate and drear!

And they, the few, have they a clearer sight
Than they the many?   Are their eyelids ope'
To some fair vision, born of faith and hope,
The which enables them to see the light?

Or are they idle dreamers by the way —
Pure visionaries who would but entice
Their souls into some fair fools' paradise,
And blind their senses to the passing day?

No doubt to those, the many, thus they seem! —
Self-hypnotized; incontinently glad;
Deluded fools, if harmless, still quite mad;
Blind to what is and sunk but in a dream!

Thus they who firm conviction ne'er have won!
Thus they with a contemptuous disdain
Affect to treat the freedom from that pain
Of discontent 'neath which they stagger on.

But if the goal of all be happiness —
Howe'er 'tis found, whatever it may be —
Why should they blind themselves, refuse to see
That others have what they, a lack, confess?

If all their efforts have but failed to bring
A firm conviction and a true content,
Why should they criticise another's bent
If not but prompted by cruel envy's sting?

What are they but blind leaders who would lead —
Not other blind — but this, the seeing eye,
Which they should rather follow and should try
From this, its harvest field, to reap some seed?

For by its fruits, so shall ye know the tree!
And that which bears a crop of discontent
Had best be left, and all our effort bent
To that which yields a calm serenity.

THE CHOICE

EACH one of us contains within his soul
A power for good or ill, for weal or woe —
Dynamic force, the which we may control
Or aimlessly permit swing to and fro.
And yet, how many sense this latent power,
Or gauge aright its mighty, dormant force,
Or dream the possibilities that dower
The life that leads it in the proper course!
The life that leads and other lives that touch
A life so led, so influenced, so inspired,
Must grow in strength (if little, or if much)
And by this hidden energy be fired —
Be fired, that is, if it be given scope,
Tended and nurtured; and if we but find
The hidden key wherewith the soul to ope',
For it ne'er comes unbidden to the mind.
Many the difficulties to o'ercome —
The deviating channels at the source
Within ourselves, that in their final sum
Deter the stream from its constructive course.
Weakness of body, spirit, or of mind,
In shielding self, would self itself betray,
By ever prompting us to search and find
Some proof to prove our own the proper way.
'Tis easier far to drift a-down the tide
Than fight the current with our puny strength,
And thus, unconsciously indeed, to glide
Into the ocean of despair at length.
'Tis easier to be weak than to be strong;

To think that we are right instead of wrong;
To feel that others but misunderstand
Who strive to stay us with a warning hand!
And this same hidden power, be it not led
Into constructive channels at its head
And source of life, must Nature's law obey
And take its course down the destructive way.
Progress or retrogression is the plan
By Nature seemingly ordained for Man!
Forward or backward!   Never standing still!
Assisting or retarding Nature's will!
Who is not for, forever 'gainst, must be!
Who is not with, must ever be without!
For Nature no neutrality can see,
Or supine indolence permit to flout.
And thus the hidden power of the soul,
If not converted to its proper use,
Soon loses individual control
And turns its force to harm, use to abuse.
For we are ever as ourselves have built;
Ours is the merit, e'en as ours the guilt;
Ours the development, or lack, of sense,
As ours the punishment or recompense!
'Tis true we carry in the blood and brain
The dormant impulse of ancestral strain
That moves to action — be it weak or strong —
Providing tendencies to right or wrong.
'Tis also true that force of circumstance
May mould or bend, if we no force oppose,
Thus making us the victims of blind chance —
The hapless dupes of her unnumbered woes!

But this, our strength, if properly applied,
Has power to overcome and quite o'erride
Those other forces — be they what they may —
And turn to use what else might but betray.
Thus are we each the product of his will;
Our strength, our weakness, what the will doth
    show;
Our good or bad, our emptiness or fill,
But normal fruits which from the will but grow!
This, then, the crop that must, indeed, sustain
Ourselves and others — be it full or light;
These our possessions — be they loss or gain,
And these our weapons in the constant fight!
And as no raindrop falls into the sea
But does thereby some other drops disturb,
So we uninfluenced can never be,
Or fail to influence — incite or curb.
And thus not only in ourselves, indeed,
But in all those who come within our life,
Our thought and action generate the seed
That comes to flower in harmony or strife!
No act of ours but leaves its full impress
Upon our own, as 'pon some other, soul,
Implanting therein courage or distress,
And thus in good or evil taking toll!
Not only word and deed, but thought as well,
In fashioning our attitude of mind,
Has power to diminish or to swell
Constructiveness in others of our kind!
Some souls are as a tonic, bringing life
And faith and hope to others on the way,

While some, absorbed in petty, selfish strife,
Themselves misled, would others cause to stray.
The one, pure gold reflecting light to all
Upon the path! The other, base alloy,
Inspiring none, but acting as a pall
To others' hope and courage, faith and joy!
Did'st ever wander in secluded glade
As evening shadows 'gin to gather round
And watch the alternating light and shade
That cast their checkered mantle on the ground?
The one, a thing of beauty, full of cheer,
Doth in the mind a confidence instil;
The other — dull, depressing, dank and drear —
Strikes to the heart its cold miasmic chill —
A blood-congealing chill that stops the flow
Of human sympathy for others' woe;
A turbid stream, polluted in its course,
That would pollute another at its source!
Thus in us all, the good with evil strives!
Ours to dispel or others' grief allay,
Or spread contamination in the lives
Of those within the orbit of our day.
'Tis ours to open or to blind the eyes!
'Tis ours to gauge, to measure and to choose!
This Nature grants; and in the grant there lies
Concealed reward, which we must win or lose!

THE EVOLUTIONARY PRINCIPLE

Through hour to day; through day to month and
    year;
Through year to generation — century;
Through age; through æon piled 'pon countless
    more —
Forgot, unnumbered in the lapse of time,
And on through countless others yet *to come;
Unchecked, unhindered by the passing day;
Converting all to its relentless sway;
The Evolutionary Principle,
Untired, untiring, still pursues its way!
Born with the birth of Time in æons past,
Whose contemplation staggers human thought,
Unceasingly it works while Time shall last
Or aught remains unfinished, or unwrought
To the perfected plan by Nature sought.
For who can count the countless ages thrown
Into the lap of Time ere yet this earth
As fiery vapor ball through space had flown —
E'en 'fore conception heralded its birth?
What countless æons must have thus elapsed!
What unimagined worlds have come and gone!
What solar systems formed, grown old, collapsed,
Ere this our little earth itself was born!
How brief is, by comparison, the time
Since this our world, grown hard and firm and
    cool,
Conceived first life in protoplasmic slime,
Beneath the evolutionary rule,

And started first upon its upward climb!
And how infinitesimal the span
'Pon this, our earth, allotted unto Man!
How late and recent must the advent be
Of this last bud 'pon the ancestral tree!
And yet, in face of this stupendous scheme,
Before the which we're lost in speechless awe,
Man, in his petty arrogance, would dream
Himself the first, and 'tempt to pick some flaw
In this, great Nature's plan, and try to prove
That, 'fore himself, naught here did live and
    move!
Himself the first creation — not the last
Of this, her process of development!
Created perfect, and his lot then cast
Into a world for his own government!
And, falling 'fore temptation's first assault,
This petty reasoning would make believe
That all men since are cursed for this, his fault,
Which no self-effort can at all retrieve,
And which divine compassion must relieve,
If but relief at all can be attained,
And that once lost be once again regained!
And in their cheap and cunning sophistry,
They make prerequisite that we believe
In this, their petty scheme, insisting that
The mind accept that which it can't receive.
And thus God-given Mind they'd prostitute
To cringing Fear, by Superstition led,
And for self-conscious thought would substitute
A thoughtless nothing, desolate and dead!

Thus do they try to bring within their ken
True Nature's God, and 'pon Him place their
      seal —
The seal and symbol of presumptuous men
Of untrained thought — bold, crude and infantile!
Thus would they dower the universal God —
The God of all that is in time or space —
With human frailties, weaknesses outgrown
E'en by the many of our time and race!
With anger, hate, revenge and petty spite;
Cruel, deceiving, arrogant and vain;
Colossal weakness and gigantic might; —
The crude conception of a savage brain!
A God who would His only son destroy
And sacrifice to His devouring lust
For blood! Whom no satiety could cloy —
Devoid of justice — worthy of no trust!
The crude conception of an early age
In human thought! A soul-defiling stain
Of human childhood, left upon the page
Of human life, and stamped upon the brain
Of each new generation by the one
That gave it birth; a relic of the dead
Passed on by each, from father unto son,
In thoughtless superstition, fear and dread!
How hard it is such precepts to outgrow
The present strength of this alone will show,
And yet to such a God as this we raise
Our thoughts in prayer, in adoration, praise;
To such a one as this we turn our eyes —
One who, if such, we must at heart despise!

[105]

And many purblind ones believe that this,
Because tradition taught, perforce must be;
And, moved by nameless terror, straightway hiss
That these same words are naught but blasphemy.
A blasphemy, indeed, thus to deny
So base a claim; to stigmatize as vain
Such crude conceptions; and, indeed, to try
To lift the vision to a higher plane!
A blasphemy to claim that Nature's God
Is not that ruthless one of fire and sword,
Revengeful lust and bloody mind and hand,
But one immeasurably just and grand!
And is not such, indeed, the God that we,
If dimly now, yet dimly still may see
O'erlooking and directing this, our way,
Through this same evolutionary sway?
How grand and mighty is the plan that thus
Unfolds itself before our wondering eyes —
A plan inspiring confidence and trust
That low to higher things must ever rise!
And Man no fallen angel here we see,
Forever expiating others' sin,
Or by another's sacrifice made free,
But one who in himself can here begin
The work which final happiness must win.
How grand the scheme that from primordial slime
Has thus developed heart and soul and mind,
And crowned with aspiration this, the climb
To greater heights — there happiness to find!
How worthy of our adoration, praise,
Is such a God — revealèd in such ways!

How worthy of our homage and our trust!
How infinitely mighty, wise and just!
And what prophetic vision can foretell
The final outcome of the mighty plan
That from the primal protoplasmic cell
Can fashion and develop conscious Man?
If in so brief a period, indeed,
Can evolution with such graces dower,
Who can forecast the bloom from this same seed
When in a later harvest come to flower?
Where'er we turn we see its mighty force
Pursuing, all unchecked, its constant course
From low to high, from high to higher still,
Controlled and guided by Infinite Will.
From mineral to plant; from plant to some
Low form of higher life the way has come!
Up, ever upward — slow, but ever sure —
And so shall come while Time shall still endure.
And on the outskirts of each kingdom we
Some close connecting link may often see;
High forms of low, low forms of high, in each,
That evolution's trend would seem to teach.
Animal life that vegetates and dies;
Unfeeling life from birth unto decline;
And vegetation that would seem to rise
To some faint sense across the border line.
And in some higher animals we find
Such indications of the heart and mind —
Of love, devotion, altruism — that
Oft put to shame the baser human kind.
But here in Man the end no doubt we reach

Of physical development at last,
Which Nature's book would seem, indeed, to teach
To be his legacy from out the past —
His legacy the which he must refine;
Must purge, develop, change from gross to fine;
And in the psychic realm advance again
Up this, the evolutionary line.
Where'er we look, the evidence we see
Of what Man was! But what he yet may be,
Who dares to say? What power can control
The upward impulse of the human soul?
The slumbering embryo within the womb
A light upon our history would cast,
And indicate from this, its living tomb,
The many stages Man has reached and passed.
From protoplasmic cell it takes its way,
Through all the lower kingdoms of the plan,
Up, ever up, unto the light of day
That breaks at last upon self-conscious Man!
What embryologist could ever see
The wonders here unfolded but must be
Convinced from this development, indeed,
That Nature's course must ever upward lead!
Does not Man's childhood, infancy and youth
The upward struggle of the race relate,
And give us living evidence, forsooth,
Of slow development from savage state?
Does not, indeed, the all-unconscious child
Suggest a being primitive and wild?
First, primal savage; then, barbarian;
Up, ever upward, unto perfect Man!

And in how many is the growth but slow!
How many lives are checked within their course!
How many grow awhile, then cease to grow
Through lack of effort at the head and source!
In individuals and nations, too,
How often is this fact indeed too true;
How often does stagnation take the place
Of active effort in life's mighty race!
For Nature has vouchsafed alone to Man
A full co-operation in her plan;
To him alone she grants the right to choose —
Advance or hinder — profit or abuse!
Each for himself must make the final choice —
For, or against, must raise his single voice —
And, having chosen, he indeed is free
To be the thing that he aspires to be.
Free, purely physical desires to tend;
Free, mental strength to nurture and to bend
To selfish aims, despising all that doth
Contribute naught to such self-centred end;
Free to develop part, instead of whole,
Of this the triune character of Man;
Or to develop body, mind and soul
In strict conformity with Nature's plan.
Those whose ambition is a selfish aim —
They who, in pandering to the senses, live —
But hinder self and abrogate their claim
To greater gifts that Nature has to give.
Self-centred creatures, grovelling in the earth
Towards some mean and petty, selfish goal,
Nor recognizing in themselves the birth,

The growth, or death, of an aspiring soul;
Servers of Self who worship at the shrine
Of Self alone, to whom they kneel and pray,
Nor note that rise has changed into decline,
And, serving Self, thus Self at last betray!
But such as these, puffed up in selfish pride,
The winnowing fans of Fate but cast aside
And leave to the converting hand of Time,
While Evolution ever up doth climb
Upon its purpose, infinite, sublime.
Within each soul the dormant power lies
To sink below or upward still to rise,
And by its effort to accelerate
The ever on and upward march of Fate.
What recompenses to be lost or gained —
What the sublimity to be attained —
He only knows who has the power to find
The limitations of the human mind.
The limitations of immortal soul —
The truth, from dim beginning to dim end —
Ultimate purpose and the final goal
Towards which all life, both high and low, doth
      tend —
Ultimates these, still far beyond our ken,
But faith intuitive must yet believe
The possibilities of There and Then
Exceed the scope of fancy to conceive.
" Imagination bodies forth," indeed,
" The forms of things unknown "; yet even they,
These fancy-flights of soul, must ever lead
Along a well defined and certain way

Marked by experience within our day.
From these encircling bounds can we be freed,
Or, far afield indeed, allowed to stray?
Can dormant mollusk, slumbering in the sand
Of ocean deeps, conceive the upper land,
Appraise the distant stretch from pole to pole,
Or gauge the depths of human mind and soul?
Can unhatched chick, within parturient shell,
Predict the comet's coming from afar,
Or spectroscopically weigh and tell
The composition of some distant star?
E'en so with us, puffed up in petty pride —
Who deeper knowledge than our own deride —
How can we say what can, or cannot, be,
Or tell what in the future may betide?
How can we plainly see while in the mesh
Of gross and slow vibrating human flesh?
How can we e'en attempt foretell the way
While bound and hampered by enclosing clay?
But we can follow step by step the tread
Of Evolution's slow but certain pace,
And note how, from amœba, it has led
Up, ever upward, to the human race.
Up, up, and ever up, the way has been;
Up, up, from low to high; from gross to fine;
With something ever higher still to win;
And what yet lies ahead — who can divine?
Our past experience at least should teach
How limitless, unmeasured and sublime
Are still the possibilities that reach
Up the long vista of Eternal Time!

CPSIA information can be obtained
at www.ICGtesting.com
Printed in the USA
BVHW040725310119
538843BV00016B/167/P